Holiness Under the Mercy Seat
by C. Matthew McMahon

Copyright Information

Holiness Under the Mercy Seat, by C. Matthew McMahon
Edited by Therese B. McMahon

Copyright ©2025 by Puritan Publications and A Puritan's Mind®

Some language and grammar have been updated from original manuscripts. Any change in wording or punctuation has not changed the intent or meaning of the original author(s) and has been made to aid the modern reader with gently updated language.

Published by Puritan Publications
A Ministry of A Puritan's Mind® in Crossville, TN.
www.apuritansmind.com
www.puritanpublications.com
www.gracechapeltn.com
www.reformedsynod.com

All rights reserved. No part of this publication may be reproduced, stored in a retrieval system or transmitted in any form by any means, electronic, mechanical, photocopy, recording or otherwise, without the prior permission of the publisher, except as provided by USA copyright law.

This Print Edition, 2025
Electronic Edition, 2025

Manufactured in the United States of America

ISBN: 978-1-62663-523-4
eISBN: 978-1-62663-522-7

Table of Contents

Introduction 4

Chapter 1: The Ark 10

Chapter 2: The Moral Law 37

Chapter 3: The Manna 66

Chapter 4: The Rod 82

Chapter 5: The Mercy Seat 99

Chapter 6: The Glory 123

Chapter 7: The Atonement 144

Chapter 8: The Wings 168

Chapter 9: The Holy Way 188

Other Works by Dr. McMahon at Puritan Publications

.... 211

Introduction

There is a sort of divine stubbornness in the Christian life—a dogged, iron-willed determination that will not be satisfied with anything less than *holiness*. A man may argue himself into all kinds of comforts, pat himself on the back for his sincerity, talk of grace and mercy with great swelling words, and yet, if he is honest with himself, he will find that there is a gnawing unrest in his soul if he is not walking rightly before God. That unrest is not the mark of the hypocrite but of the child of God who has forgotten where his refuge lies. He knows, somewhere deep down, that Christ did not save him to remain as he was. The throne of grace was not thrown open to allow men to wallow in the filth of their sins, but to make them clean, to place them in the shelter of the Almighty, to set them under the mercy seat, where the blood of sprinkling speaks better things than that of Abel.

This book is about that great theme—holiness under the mercy seat. The phrase itself carries weight, for it immediately calls to mind the ark of the covenant, the throne of God's grace in the Old Testament, the place where the High Priest entered but once a year, trembling, to make atonement for the sins of the people. That mercy seat, covered in blood, overshadowed by the wings of the cherubim, was the most holy place in all the earth. And yet, it was only a shadow. It was a token of what was to come, for now, Christ has entered into the true holy place, into heaven itself, where He ever lives to make intercession for

His people. And so, holiness under the mercy seat is not a mere theological concept; it is the very heart of the Christian life. It is the doctrine of living before God in light of Christ's atonement, of walking in obedience, of serving the living God with a conscience purified by His blood.

The book before you is not concerned with vague generalities or empty platitudes. It is not the kind of work that pats the reader on the head and tells him that all is well, no matter how he lives (*most* of the contemporary church operates on that plane). It is the kind of book that takes a man by the collar, sits him down, and tells him plainly what God requires. And the requirements are not small. The book does not deal in the currency of modern religious sentiment, where grace is treated as a hall pass for sin and holiness as an optional extra for the exceptionally devout. No, it stands in the long line of biblical teaching that says, *"Follow peace with all men, and holiness, without which no man shall see the Lord,"* (Hebrews 12:14). It insists that the Christian life is not a casual thing, but a life lived in the shadow of the mercy seat, under the blood of Christ, in the presence of the living God.

The foundation of the book is laid (as you will see further along in reading) with Psalm 61:4: *"I will abide in thy tabernacle for ever: I will trust in the covert of thy wings."* From this idea, the first chapter unfolds the great desire of the believer, which is to dwell in the presence of God, to find refuge under the shadow of His wings as seen by the ark. David, when pursued by enemies, did not merely wish for relief from danger, but for the assurance that he was safe in God's care. And where did he look for that safety? To the mercy seat, to the place of atonement, to the very dwelling place of God among His people. The book traces this theme through the whole of Scripture, showing that the believer's true refuge is not found in his own strength, nor in the fleeting securities of this world, but in Christ, in the covenant promises of God, in the sure and steadfast hope that anchors the soul.

The doctrine that flows from this is clear: God's love and protection in Christ is found under the mercy seat. The work builds upon Hebrews 9:14: *"How much more shall the blood of Christ, who through the eternal Spirit offered himself without spot to God, purge your conscience from dead works to serve the living God?"* The contrast between dead works and true service is at the core of what it means to walk in holiness. Dead works, those vain attempts to please God apart from Christ, are set against the true and living way that He has opened for His people. Holiness is not a grim duty, nor a mere outward show, but the necessary effect of being under the mercy seat, the natural consequence of being redeemed by the blood of Christ.

From here, the book moves into the practical outworking of these truths. It examines what it means to come before God in worship, not with a dead and lifeless formality, but with a conscience purified, with a heart sprinkled clean. It calls to mind passages like Psalm 93:5: *"Holiness becometh thine house, O Lord, for ever."* Worship is not a casual affair; it is an approach to the living God, a drawing near to the throne of grace with reverence and godly fear. And yet, this is not a fear that drives the believer away, but one that draws him closer. He comes boldly, not because he is worthy, but because Christ has made the way. He stands under the mercy seat, not trembling as the High Priest once did, but with confidence, because his Great High Priest has gone before him.

At the heart of this work is the reality that holiness is not a burdensome requirement, but the very life of the Christian. It is not a condition that must be met, in order to earn God's favor, but the inevitable result of having received it. As Romans 6:22 says, *"But now being made free from sin, and become servants to God, ye have your fruit unto holiness, and the end everlasting life."* The Christian is no longer a servant of sin; he has been freed, not to live for himself, but to live unto God. This is where the book presses upon the reader most directly. It asks, in no uncertain terms, *What are you most distressed about?* Are you concerned with holiness? Are you troubled by your own coldness, by your sluggishness in the things of God, by the dullness of your affections? Or are you content to drift, to speak lightly of grace while neglecting the life it demands?

The book does not allow you, reader, to escape into comfortable excuses. It does not present holiness as an unattainable ideal, nor as a heavy yoke. Instead, it presents it as the necessary and joyful consequence of belonging to Christ. It draws on passages like Colossians 1:13: *"Who hath delivered us from the power of darkness, and hath translated us into the kingdom of his dear Son."* The Christian is not merely improved; he is a new creation, brought into a new kingdom, set under a new rule. And in that kingdom, holiness is not an option—it is the very air he breathes.

And yet, the book does not fall into the trap of making holiness a thing of mere effort. It does not burden the reader with law while stripping away the gospel. Rather, it constantly draws the reader back to the mercy seat, to the throne of grace, to Christ Himself. It reminds him that all his sufficiency is in Christ, that he is upheld not by his own striving, but by the power of God. As Philippians 2:13 declares, *"For it is God which worketh in you both to will and to do of his good pleasure."* The believer's holiness is not ultimately his own work—it is the work of Christ in him.

The book ends where it must—with an exhortation to steadfastness. Holiness is not a momentary enthusiasm; it is the life of the believer. It is the proof that he belongs to Christ, the evidence that he is under the mercy seat, the mark that he is truly redeemed. It is no small thing to be a Christian. It is no light matter to be called a child of God. The world, the flesh, and the devil will do all they can to shake the believer from his place, to make him forget his refuge, to lure him away from the mercy seat. But the call remains: *"The Lord knoweth them that are his,"* (2 Timothy 2:19). And those who are His will endure, for He will keep them. He will shelter them under His wings. He will preserve them in holiness. And in the end, they will see Him as He is, and they will be like Him.

This book is a call to that life—to live beneath the mercy seat, to walk in holiness, to serve the living God. And it does not call the reader to this in his own strength, but in the strength of Christ, under the shadow of His wings, in the safety of His everlasting covenant. It is a book worth reading, worth meditating on, and, most importantly, worth living.

In Christ's grace and mercy,
C. Matthew McMahon, Ph.D., Th.D.
From My study, February, 2025
"...search the Scriptures..." (John 5:39).
www.apuritansmind.com
www.puritanpublications.com
www.gracechapeltn.com
www.reformedsynod.com

Chapter 1: The Ark

"And I will give you pastors according to mine heart, which shall feed you with knowledge and understanding. And it shall come to pass, when ye be multiplied and increased in the land, in those days, saith the LORD, they shall say no more, The ark of the covenant of the LORD: neither shall it come to mind: neither shall they remember it; neither shall they visit it; neither shall that be done any more," (Jeremiah 3:15-16).

Of all the subjects a faithful preacher of the Gospel must proclaim, there is both great delight and immense benefit in considering the *types* that reveal the mysteries of the Gospel to the church found in the Old Testament. Such study requires distinguishing between shadow and substance, *rightly* dividing the word of truth. The Scriptures testify of Jesus Christ, and His work, ministry, and teaching are present throughout the Old Testament, which was referred to as *the Scriptures* even before the New Testament was written. Most Christians forget that Jesus' bible was the Old Testament.

The Old Testament is rich with types, filled with grace, yet veiled in shadows—shadows that persisted until they were utterly scattered by the coming of Jesus Christ, the Messiah. These types are no longer veiled in ignorance but are revealed in full understanding, rightly divided by the light of Christ. The removal of these silhouettes is inevitable, for as the full and perfect day approaches, shadows *must* fade. The higher the sun rises, the shorter the shadows grow, until at noon they are nearly gone. Likewise, all shadows will vanish, just as the shadows of the Law fled at Christ's first coming, "Which are a shadow of things to come; but the body is of Christ," (Colossians 2:17). Though they once darkened the church in times past, when the day of the Lord appears, they will no longer be remembered or spoken of, as God Himself testifies in Jeremiah 3:16.

In his second sermon, Jeremiah speaks of divorce and adultery, disobedience and destruction, as they relate to the people of God. The imagery of divorce, following the commandment God gave on Sinai, "Thou shalt not commit adultery," (Exodus 20:14), is not merely physical but spiritual, illustrating how the northern and southern kingdoms were *unfaithful* to God. Jeremiah portrays God's relationship with His people as that of an innocent husband, warning His adulterous wife of *a great divorce*, yet longing to restore the broken marriage out of His great love for her.

This passage, particularly Jeremiah 3:12-25, which includes our primary text, contains an invitation to return to the Lord based on repentance from spiritual adultery. The Lord appeals to His people, calling them to confess and renounce their grievous sins of idolatry and unfaithfulness so that they might be restored. He promises that if they return, He will bless them and heal their wayward hearts. The call to repentance in these opening verses serves as the foundation for the larger passage from Jeremiah 3:1 through

4:4. Verses 12-13 extend an offer of repentance to Israel, while verses 14-15 extend the same call to Judah.

They are called "backsliding children," but *backsliding* is not merely a temporary lapse in judgment or a momentary weakness. It is a *deliberate departure* from God, a headlong fall toward destruction apart from repentance. Many presume backsliding to be a *minor* moral failing, yet in Scripture, it is often marked by giving oneself over to idolatry, a sign of reprobation if repentance does not follow.

In verse 15, the Lord declares that He will give His repentant people shepherds after His own heart—teachers, pastors, and rulers who will lead them rightly. True repentance is accompanied by proper government under God's kingship in Zion, as opposed to the corrupt rule of earthly authorities. In contrast, Jeremiah 2:8 speaks of evil "rulers" or "shepherds," using the same word that appears in Jeremiah 3:15, but there it refers to those who led the people *astray*. The promise of restoration is given, but only under the condition that the people turn to God in repentance. "And it shall come to pass, when ye be multiplied and increased in the land, in those days, saith the LORD, they shall say no more, The ark of the covenant of the LORD: neither shall it come to mind: neither shall they remember it; neither shall they visit it; neither shall that be done any more," (Jeremiah 3:16).

There is then a mention in verse 16 of the *ark* of the covenant. The ark was the central point of worship in both the tabernacle and the temple. Covenant was at the heart of its purpose, for it represented the binding agreement between God and His people. It was the place of God's presence, where He was enthroned as King. The ark was His *throne*, the mercy seat His seat of rule. The cherubim's outstretched wings formed a covering above the ark, marking the place where God was said to dwell (*sit*). He was enthroned between the cherubim, ruling over His people in mercy and justice.

It was also the place of God's rule in the context of redemption. "And it shall come to pass in the last days, that the mountain of the LORD'S house shall be established in the top of the mountains, and shall be exalted above the hills; and all nations shall flow unto it. And many people shall go and say, Come ye, and let us go up to the mountain of the LORD, to the house of the God of Jacob; and he will teach us of his ways, and we will walk in his paths: for out of Zion shall go forth the law, and the word of the LORD from Jerusalem," (Isaiah 2:2-3). The ark, once central to the worship of Israel, would be displaced, and the covenant of faith *fulfilled*.[1] The rule of God would go forth from Zion—not through an object hidden behind a veil but from the very hearts of His people, in whom He would dwell. The veil would be removed, and all would be made manifest.

The ark of the covenant was first introduced in its making:

---

[1] Yes, that covenant of faith is the covenant at Sinai. Sinai was *no* covenant of works.

"And they shall make an ark of shittim wood: two cubits and a half shall be the length thereof, and a cubit and a half the breadth thereof, and a cubit and a half the height thereof. And thou shalt overlay it with pure gold, within and without shalt thou overlay it, and shalt make upon it a crown of gold round about. And thou shalt cast four rings of gold for it, and put them in the four corners thereof; and two rings shall be in the one side of it, and two rings in the other side of it. And thou shalt make staves of shittim wood, and overlay them with gold. And thou shalt put the staves into the rings by the sides of the ark, that the ark may be borne with them. The staves shall be in the rings of the ark: they shall not be taken from it. And thou shalt put into the ark the testimony which I shall give thee. And thou shalt make a mercy seat of pure gold: two cubits and a half shall be the length thereof, and a cubit and a half the breadth thereof. And thou shalt make two cherubims of gold, of beaten work shalt thou make them, in the two ends of the mercy seat. And make one cherub on the one end, and the other cherub on the other end: even of the mercy seat shall ye make the cherubims on the two ends thereof. And the cherubims shall stretch forth their wings on high, covering the mercy seat with their wings, and their faces shall look one to another; toward the mercy seat shall the faces of the cherubims be. And thou shalt put the mercy seat above upon the ark; and in the ark thou shalt put the testimony that I shall give thee. And there I will meet with thee, and I will commune with thee from above the mercy seat, from between the two cherubims which are upon the ark of the testimony, of all things which I will give thee in commandment unto the children of Israel," (Exodus 25:10-22).

God was very precise in how the ark was to be fashioned, for it served as the earthly representation of His throne.

In this passage in Jeremiah, there is an anticipation of a Messianic age in which the ark would *no longer* have a role in earthly worship. When repentance takes hold, and when God establishes true shepherds and pastors over His people, there will no longer be a need for an ark to remain hidden behind a veil in the temple. "The ark of the covenant of the Lord," would no longer be spoken of as the center of worship, for God's communion with His people would not be confined to a physical object. Instead, *Zion* would become the central place of His presence. The ark would no longer be His throne, for His dominion would extend far beyond the confines of a single nation. He would be enthroned in the hearts of all His people, ruling in mercy and righteousness from within. The church, clothed in an alien righteousness that depends wholly on Christ, is a far more glorious throne than the mercy seat concealed behind a veil.

In the age of the Messiah, these blessings would be fully realized. God would provide shepherds for His people, men wholly devoted to Him, as He declared: "men after mine own heart." Such pastors would love what He loves, teach what He commands, and lead His people according to His will. Any who *fail* to do so are imposters and not sent by Him. Throughout history, there were godly leaders—Moses, Ezra, Nehemiah, Joshua, Isaiah, Jeremiah—but they were merely forerunners of the One who would fulfill all things. Even Moses testified of this coming Prophet: "The LORD thy God will raise up unto thee a Prophet from the midst of thee, of thy brethren, like unto me; unto him ye shall hearken," (Deuteronomy 18:15). The full truth of this prophecy was revealed only in the promised Messiah, the chief Shepherd and Bishop of souls, and in the apostles whom He appointed as teachers in Zion.

A new and greater *form* of worship would be introduced. The ark, once the centerpiece of the ceremonial system, would be *fulfilled*, and it would not be missed. The presence of God among His people would be known in the person of Jesus Christ. "And it shall come to pass... they shall say no more, The ark of the covenant of the LORD," (Jeremiah 3:16).

Jeremiah's preaching was addressed to *a faithless people*—a word he repeats often throughout his prophecy. Yet despite their unfaithfulness, God offered forgiveness and restoration to those who would acknowledge their sin and repent. "Only acknowledge thine iniquity, that thou hast transgressed against the LORD thy God," (Jeremiah 3:13). The merciful love of the Father stands in stark contrast to the bleak backdrop of idolatry and spiritual adultery, which is nothing less than *apostasy*. And the unthinkable would occur: the ark of the covenant, once the very heart of Israel's worship, would no longer even be mentioned. The age to come would be one in which the Son of God would reign from His heavenly mercy seat, interceding and ruling forever.

Doctrine: *The ark of the covenant is a type of the fulfillment of the work of God's Christ.*

Moses was first shown the patterns of the things the tabernacle was to contain—the ark, the table of shewbread, and the seven-branched candlestick, or lampstand, along with all its accessories. Each of these held significance, but the ark stood at the center, representing the very presence of God among His people.

In the holy of holies, into which the high priest entered only once a year, there were distinct levels of religious service in the temple. Hourly, there was attendance in the outer courts, where many stood watch through all hours of the day and night. Daily, there was attendance in the holy place, where the lighting of lamps and the burning of incense were performed. Weekly, there was attendance where fresh shewbread was set before the Lord every Sabbath. And once a year, in the most holy place, the high priest alone entered that secret chamber to make atonement for the sins of the people. Upon the hem of his garments were bells, and interwoven among them were pomegranates—symbols of the sweetness of his work and the activity of his intercession. There, in the presence of

God, he sprinkled the blood of atonement upon the mercy seat.

The temple itself was small, yet it was filled with sacred and mysterious furnishings. Inside its walls was the holy place, not large by any standard, and within it was an even smaller chamber—the holy of holies. And in that sacred space stood an object of the highest importance—a square chest, an *ark*. This golden ark contained the tablets of the law, signifying covenant and communion, the golden pot of manna, representing God's provision, and Aaron's rod that budded, a sign of life brought forth from death.[2] The blood of atonement was sprinkled upon this ark, and year after year, God's presence consumed that blood, signifying the removal of wrath. As the writer to the Hebrews declares, these three items within the ark all pointed to God's covenant dealings with His people.

The ark itself was a chest or box, measuring three feet nine inches long, two feet three inches wide, and two feet three inches deep. It was overlaid with pure gold, with an ornamental molding along the top, like a *crown*. Four rings of gold were affixed to its lower corners—its bases—so that it might be carried without being touched. The ark was borne upon poles made of shittim wood, carried by the priests or Levites upon their shoulders. These poles were inserted into the rings of the ark, yet they were not part of

---

[2] There is some commentary *contention* as to the way the three objects associated with the ark were laid (in or out of the ark). But this argues beyond our "practical intention" in our study.

the ark itself, ensuring that no human hand would come into direct contact with what was most holy.

The ark contained the testimony of God—the Decalogue, the two tablets of stone, written by the very finger of God, declaring His law and testifying against sin. As a cover upon the ark was the mercy seat, above which stood two cherubim, their wings stretched high. Their faces were turned toward one another, yet both looked downward upon the mercy seat, as guardians of the covenant, overshadowing the law and the place of atonement. Their wings formed a throne, a seat of divine majesty.

And it was here, in this sacred place, that God declared, "I will meet with thee." The purpose of the ark was to provide a place where God might reveal Himself in *holiness* to His people. It was the appointed place of *communion*, where the presence of God rested above the mercy seat, between the cherubim, and above the ark of the covenant. Here, in glory, God met with His people.

The symbolism of the ark of the covenant may be considered either separately, in relation to its individual parts, or collectively, in how these parts relate to one another.

Individually, the ark consisted of three primary elements: the ark itself, the mercy seat with its *crown*, and the golden cherubim. The ark, made of acacia or shittim wood and overlaid with pure gold, was designed to house the law written *by* the finger of God. It represented God's divine covenant, His authoritative testimony, and His power to restore what was lost through the fall. The divine law, preserved within the pure nature of God, was mirrored in the materials used. Acacia wood, known for its durability, symbolized incorruptibility, while gold, the most precious and enduring of metals, signified the unchanging and perfect righteousness of God. "Wherefore the law is holy, and the commandment holy, and just, and good," (Romans 7:12). The law of God, which is holy, just, and good, required a vessel that reflected His perfect nature—an unbending, immutable, and incorruptible testimony of His righteousness.

The mercy seat (aptly named), placed above the ark, represented God's *mercy*. Just as He covers the sins of His people, the mercy seat covered the law. Blood was sprinkled upon it, signifying the sacrificial work of Christ, who is the true propitiation for sin. The law, which declared judgment, was placed beneath the covering of mercy. The cherubim, fashioned in gold, represented both protection *and* worship. Their presence signified watchfulness over the holy place and the intense sanctity of God's dwelling. Their outstretched wings hovered over the mercy seat, demonstrating their protective charge, while their bowed heads and downward-facing eyes signified reverence. Even these representations of angelic beings did not look upon God directly. Instead, their gaze was fixed upon the place of atonement, illustrating that even angels desire to look into the mystery of redemption, "which things the angels desire to look into," (1 Peter 1:12). The cherubim, lost in awe at

God's mercy, watched in wonder at how Christ's atonement would reverse the curse of the fall.

Considered together, the ark's symbolism speaks to the meeting of divine attributes, as David declares, "Mercy and truth are met together; righteousness and peace have kissed each other," (Psalm 85:10). The law, kept in the most sacred place, testified to God's holiness, while the mercy seat, covering the law, declared that mercy was superior in God's redemptive plan. The cherubim, peering down in amazement, reflected the wonder of heaven at the union of mercy and justice through a substitutionary atonement—an offering both pleasing to God and satisfying His righteous demands. Through this, mankind is brought into communion with God.

The ark, the mercy seat, and the cherubim, once placed within the holy of holies, were *hidden* from the public eye. In the days of the tabernacle, the Levites carried the ark from place to place, and the people may have seen its procession. However, once the temple was built, the ark was set behind stone walls and a veil too thick to be seen through. The place of communion was concealed, veiled from common sight. The cherubim, in this role, (recall the guardians of Eden), stood at the entrance after man's expulsion. Just as they barred the way to the tree of life with a flaming sword, so they guarded the way into the presence of God. Yet in the ark, there was no sword. Redemption had transformed their role. No longer were they the wardens of judgment, but now they were figures of contemplation, overshadowing the mercy seat, associated with the work of reconciliation. "There is joy in the presence of the angels of God over one sinner that repenteth," (Luke 15:10). Through Christ, the way back into God's presence was no longer barred, peace was restored, and communion was granted. The cherubim, once stationed to keep man from Eden, now bore witness to the redemption that made reconciliation possible. They stand as ministering spirits, beholding with joy the work of God in restoring sinners to Himself.

In the place where the Lord meets and communes with His people, the ark held the *testimony* of His *covenant*. Meeting with God must be on His terms, where righteousness and sin are confronted. There is no communion with God if either is disregarded, and no approach to Him apart from the way He has prescribed.

The ark served as the chest in which the testimony of God was kept, sealing up that which was sure and even hidden: "The secret of the LORD is with them that fear him; and he will shew them his covenant," (Psalm 25:14). Within this ark was the rod of discipline for the sinner (Aaron's rod or stick), the manna for the repentant, and the law for all. The ark, in its fullness, signified the heart of the believer within the tabernacle—that is, the church. Within that ark dwelled the covenant of God, which was later declared in Jeremiah: "But this shall be the covenant that I will make with the house of Israel; After those days, saith the LORD, I will put my law in their inward parts, and write it in their hearts; and will be their God, and they shall be my people," (Jeremiah 31:33). Those who belong to God are secure within the ark, just as the ark is secure within them—a testimony to the work of redemption.

It is called the Ark of God, (1 Samuel 3:3). The Ark of the Lord, (Joshua 3:13). The Ark of the Covenant of the Lord, (Numbers 10:33). The Ark of His Strength, (Psalm 132:8). The Ark of the Testimony, (Numbers 4:5). The Glory of Israel, (1 Samuel 4:21-22). In the New Testament, it is referenced as the Ark of the Testament in Revelation 11:19: "And there was seen in his temple the ark of his testament." The temple alone is not revealed, but the ark itself—once shut away from the eyes of men in the holy of holies, concealed from view even from the high priest except on rare occasions (1 Kings 6:19)—is now *opened*. The mysteries once hidden are now revealed, seen in heaven itself, for the ark represents God's throne.

The ark was the sacred chest that contained the two tablets of the law, the foundation of the *covenant of faith* between God and His people (Exodus 26:3). Aaron's rod and the golden pot of manna were also placed within, as a witness to His faithfulness (Exodus 25:21). Above it was the mercy seat, which foreshadowed Christ, the true means of atonement in that covenant. The ark, hidden behind the veil, typified Christ's flesh, which concealed His divine nature: "Having therefore, brethren, boldness to enter into the holiest by the blood of Jesus, by a new and living way, which he hath consecrated for us, through the veil, that is to say, his flesh," (Hebrews 10:19-20).

Christ is the true ark of the covenant, the fulfillment of all that it represented. In Him is atonement with the

Father, declared, preached, and proclaimed as the only way of reconciliation. In heaven, the ark is seen in its true form, where the saints, in perfect joy, behold the face of God in Christ. This is the true ark—not that the Old Testament ark was false, but that it was a *type* destined to pass away in due time.

Christ Himself testified that all of the Old Testament spoke of Him. "For had ye believed Moses, ye would have believed me: for he wrote of me," (John 5:46). Moses bore witness to Christ through promises, prophecies, and through figures and shadows, such as the ark. Had the Jews believed Moses, they would have also believed in Jesus, for the rites and ordinances given to them pointed unmistakably to the Messiah. If they had rightly considered the purpose behind these ordinances, they would have realized that none were unnecessary, for all of them anticipated Christ. "And it shall come to pass, when ye be multiplied and increased in the land, in those days, saith the LORD, they shall say no more, The ark of the covenant of the LORD: neither shall it come to mind: neither shall they remember it; neither shall they visit it; neither shall that be done any more," (Jeremiah 3:16). Why is this so? Because the Lord Jesus, through His redemptive work, fulfills all that the ark foreshadowed. So completely does He fulfill it that the ark itself fades from worship, its purpose finished. The new covenant in Christ replaces the old (that new covenant which started in Genesis 3:15), for He is the true ark, the final atonement, the fulfillment of all that was promised.

God, in His wisdom, veiled the glory of Christ's kingdom for a time, presenting it in *shadows* and *figures*. He prepared a people through piety and holiness, stirring within them an awareness of sin and a longing for mercy. To this end, He appointed sacrifices, ceremonies, and symbols to declare what Christ would ultimately accomplish. In the fullness of time, Christ did not abolish these things, but He brought them to their intended fulfillment. In Him, they are no longer obscure, but made clear. He trained His people through these types, teaching them to give thanks for His mercy and to see themselves as those who commune with Him through grace.

The ark represented the covenant of God in sacred things, pointing directly to Christ. It contained both elements and circumstances—elements referring to the essential parts of God's ordained worship, such as the ark itself in the Old Testament, and circumstances referring to lesser details, such as the *time* in which the high priest entered the holy of holies. The essential elements were necessary: the sacraments, the sacrifices, the prescribed means of communion with God. Circumstances, such as an extra moment spent in the holy of holies on the Day of Atonement, were not of equal weight. Through sacrifice, believers approached God, presenting their duty to Him by faith in the one true Mediator. Outward signs, seals, and confirmations testified to the promises of grace, reinforcing God's word by visible means.

Even in the beginning, God used signs to confirm His covenant. Before the fall, He established a *covenant of works*

Chapter 1: The Ark

with Adam, offering life on the condition of perfect obedience. Yet He did not leave Adam without signs—He appointed the tree of life and the tree of the knowledge of good and evil as visible witnesses. After the fall, He continued this pattern. He gave His word and then provided outward seals of His covenant, establishing circumcision and the Passover as signs of grace in the old dispensation.

Under the new covenant, these promises are fulfilled in Christ, and now the gospel is proclaimed to all who believe in His name—crucified, buried, risen, ascended, and reigning at the right hand of the Father. The sacraments of baptism and the Lord's Supper now serve as the visible seals of this completed covenant.

Thus, the Lord has always spoken through both His word and His signs, appointing them as means of instruction and assurance. The ark, in all its meaning, was a type—a figure pointing toward Christ. Now that He has come, all its significance is found in Him. The covenant, once housed in a golden chest, is now written on the hearts of His people. The mercy seat, once hidden behind a veil, is now openly revealed in the person of Christ, who intercedes for His people. The presence of God, once localized within the temple, now fills the hearts of all who trust in Him. The ark was a shadow, but Christ is the substance.

Joseph Bellamy describes the ark's significance: "The whole law of Moses, which was written in a book, comprises at large all the contents of the covenant with the Israelites in the wilderness. This book, therefore, was called the book of the covenant. And the little chest in which it was put, from the special use to which it was appropriated, was called the Ark of the covenant. A brief summary of this law was written on two tables of stone. Which two tables of stone were, therefore, called the tables of the covenant, and were also put into the Ark of the covenant. So that we may be as certain of the nature of that covenant, as we can be of the meaning of the Mosaic law."[3] The ark held the covenant, the tangible expression of God's law and testimony. It was the center of Israel's worship, the place where God's presence was manifested among His people. The most holy place in the temple *typified* heaven itself. The ark signified the covenant and the security found within it, as the heart of divine influence in worship. The ark was a special type of Christ and His work, for in Him are hidden all the treasures of wisdom and knowledge: "In whom [*that is, Jesus*] are hid all the treasures of wisdom and knowledge," (Colossians 2:3). The Father gives His testimony—His covenant—to His people, and only those who receive it by repentance will partake in its blessings.

The construction of the ark itself pointed to the nature of Christ. Wood on the inside and gold on the outside—His humanity and divinity. *Crowned* with gold, it displayed the exalted Son, showing forth the glory of His work and the crowning achievement of His redemptive mission. God made the ark the most sacred representation of His presence in the Old Testament, dwelling above the

---

[3] Joseph Bellamy, *The Works of Joseph Bellamy*, vol. 3, n.d. (New York: Stephen Dodge, 1812) 140.

mercy seat, in the midst of His people, in the holy of holies, the heart of the temple. Where the ark was, there was the name of the Lord of hosts, who dwelt between the cherubim. There, in sacrifice and blood, communion was granted. Holiness and covenant were central.

During the wilderness journey, the ark went before the people, leading them in their pilgrimage (Numbers 10:33). When they settled, it remained in their midst, the focal point of their worship. It was the place where God promised to commune with His people, where prayer and sacrifice were accepted. This typified the Father's perfect satisfaction in the work of His Son, the beloved in whom He is well pleased. What could be more precious than Christ? And what was more precious to Israel than the ark?

The ark, as a type, reflected the *glory* of Christ. The visible presence of God was witnessed in the ark and its service. "And it came to pass, when the priests were come out of the holy place, that the cloud filled the house of the LORD," (1 Kings 8:11). This visible glory, radiant and full of light, signified the brilliance of God's presence. Likewise, Christ will come to His people in glory, the fulfillment of the covenant. "When Christ, who is our life, shall appear, then shall ye also appear with him in glory," (Colossians 3:4). The ark was a testimony to God's presence, a sign of how greatly He esteemed communion with His people, which is called His glory (Romans 9:4, 15).

The Ark and the Day of Atonement

The ark was the central point of the Day of Atonement, though this will be explored in greater detail later. Blood was sprinkled upon the ark: "So shall he sprinkle many nations," (Isaiah 52:15). This signified Christ's work—He would sprinkle the nations with the doctrine of the gospel, converting many through the power of the Spirit. His atoning blood would sanctify and cleanse, purifying the conscience from sin. "Having our hearts sprinkled from an evil conscience," (Hebrews 10:20). The ceremonial act of sprinkling blood upon the mercy seat found its true fulfillment in Christ, who cleanses the hearts of believers by His Spirit.

The prophets spoke of this cleansing work: "I will sprinkle clean water upon you, and ye shall be clean," (Ezekiel 36:25). This was the promise of the covenant, a declaration of pardon and reconciliation, sealed by the blood of Christ. "And to the blood of sprinkling," (Hebrews 12:24). As the ark was once sprinkled with blood, now Christ, in its *fulfillment*, sprinkles His people with His own blood, confirming the new covenant as its Mediator. The entire ceremonial system has passed away, for Christ has fulfilled every part of the law.

The sprinkling upon the ark pointed to the true faith, the application of Christ's merit to the soul. "Let us draw near with a true heart in full assurance of faith, having our hearts sprinkled from an evil conscience, and our bodies washed with pure water," (Hebrews 10:22). In the Old Testament, anointing was a sign of consecration, and those anointed were set apart for service to God. This was fulfilled in Christ, the Anointed One, who now anoints His people by His Spirit in greater measure. "Through the sprinkling of the blood of Jesus Christ," (1 Peter 1:2).

Why Was an Ark Necessary?

The ark was necessary because of the holiness of God, and Christ was necessary because such service must be fulfilled to the Father in perfect holiness. And yet, as the text declares, "The ark of the covenant of the Lord... neither shall it come to mind," (Jeremiah 3:16). The presence of the Lord with His church now surpasses what was once known, for the ark will no longer be remembered. The old ceremonies were not to be altered by the Jewish people, but by God, who designed to bring them to completion in Christ. The law was established for a time, and no longer.

Jeremiah's words are clear: "In those days... they shall say no more, the ark of the covenant of the Lord," (Jeremiah 3:16). The ceremonial law will no longer be valued as before. No one will request its return, for Christ has come. Those who seek to reintroduce the ceremonies reject Christ's finished work, turning from Christian worship to superstition. The prophet Daniel foresaw this change, declaring that the Messiah would bring an end to sacrifices (Daniel 9:27).

All the promises of the Father concerning worship pointed *to Christ and His kingdom*. The Old Testament prophecies about Zion's future glory refer not to a rebuilt temple, but to the reign of Christ in His church. The ceremonial law, the ark of the covenant, and all its symbols have been *dissolved*, for Christ has *fulfilled* them. The gospel, once shown in types and figures, is now revealed in its fullness. The most holy place was a shadow of Christ, the true dwelling place of God.

The ark of the covenant is a type of the fulfillment of the work of God's Christ. He alone takes away sin and brings everlasting righteousness. His holiness surpasses all, for He is the fulfillment of what the ark only signified.

The ark as a *type* presses you to consider your service and worship to Christ. If you desire God to prosper what you have and to bless your labor in His service, then you must seek the grace to serve Him. The blessings and curses outlined in Deuteronomy 28 make it clear that the covenant relationship between God and His people brings either favor or judgment. Consider the house of Obed-Edom, where the Ark of the Covenant rested for a time. "So David would not remove the ark of the LORD unto him into the city of David: but David carried it aside into the house of Obededom the Gittite. And the ark of the LORD continued in the house of Obededom the Gittite three months: and the LORD blessed Obededom, and all his household," (2 Samuel 6:10-11). The presence of God brought blessing. Was God in Obed-Edom's house before? Not like this. His dwelling brought *a unique prosperity*. Now, consider: if the mere presence of the ark could bring such blessing, how much more will you be blessed when God Himself, by His Spirit, dwells within you? If the ark brought temporary favor, how much greater is the favor of the indwelling Christ? His presence is in you by faith, a presence that far surpasses the old ways. The ark is gone, but Christ remains. And where He is esteemed, where His holiness is cherished, there, grace is poured out in abundance.

Gospel Worship is Greater Worship

"In those days, saith the Lord, (that is, in the days of Messiah) they shall no more say, the ark of the covenant of the Lord, neither shall it come to mind, neither shall they remember it, neither shall that be done any more." The ark was the heart of Old Testament worship, but it was never meant to be permanent. There is a figure of speech in this passage, where a part is used to stand for the whole. The ark represents all the legal ceremonies—the entire sacrificial system of the Old Covenant. The meaning is plain: when Christ comes, the whole system will cease, for He fulfills *every part* of it. The ark contained the pot of manna, Aaron's rod, and the tables of the law. Christ is all these things. He is the true manna, the bread of life. He is the rod of government, ruling His people with perfect righteousness. And in Him, the whole law is fulfilled, for He is the living Word of God. Since Christ now reigns in His church by His Word and Spirit, all the former things that pertained to the ceremonies must cease.

The Spirit of God was given in the Old Testament but in a lesser measure. In those days, only a select few received the Spirit explicitly, and even then, it was only in part. Comparatively, it was said that the Spirit was "not yet given" (John 7:39), for the great outpouring was reserved for after Christ's ascension. The fullness of the Spirit's gifts, graces, and blessings was reserved for the Gospel age. It was promised: "And it shall come to pass afterward, that I will pour out my spirit upon all flesh," (Joel 2:28). What was once given in small measure is now poured out abundantly. No more ark. No more ceremonies. Now, all of Christ's benefits flow freely, an endless stream from a fountain that never runs dry.

During the Old Testament, God appeared in thick darkness (1 Kings 8:10-12). Paul tells us that in the New Covenant, God is manifest in the flesh. The glory of God, once hidden behind veils and ceremonies, has now been fully revealed in Christ. The mercy seat, once placed upon the Ark of the Covenant in the Holy of Holies, was a *shadow* of Christ. Paul says He was "justified in the Spirit," (Romans 4:25). His resurrection declared Him the true atonement, the perfect fulfillment of the Father's will. The tables of the law, once sealed in the ark, were fulfilled in Him.

The cherubim overshadowing the mercy seat symbolized God's glory. Angels bore witness to Christ, just as they stood at the empty tomb, declaring His resurrection (Matthew 28:2). The ark was a sign of the Messiah who was to come, and now Christ has been preached among the nations. "But I say, Have they not heard? Yes verily, their sound went into all the earth, and their words unto the ends of the world," (Romans 10:18). The truth of the ark—God's presence, His covenant, His redemption—has now gone out into the world in the message of Christ.

The visible appearance of God was once rare. The high priest entered the Holy of Holies only once a year. But now, Christ has been revealed. "And without controversy great is the mystery of godliness: God was manifest in the flesh, justified in the Spirit, seen of angels, preached unto the Gentiles, believed on in the world, received up into glory," (1 Timothy 3:16). Though He has ascended, He remains present with His people through the Spirit until the end of the age.

The Greater Glory of the Gospel

The Gospel is more glorious than Adam's old covenant. The Father made Himself known before Christ came, but in the revelation of the Gospel, His word is clearer and more radiant. The Law was a shadow, the Gospel is its full manifestation. The Law was glorious as a mirror reflecting God's character, but the Gospel is the light itself. Moses' face shone when he received the law, but even that glory faded. The Gospel never fades.

Christ has fulfilled all that the law required. The moral law remains glorious, but now it is seen in its fullness, as Christ is the true ark who has satisfied its demands. If the ark was revered, how much more should we esteem Christ? If the presence of the ark brought blessing, how much more should we desire the presence of Christ? If the ark demanded reverence, how much more should our hearts be filled with awe at the one who now reigns over all?

The question before you is this: do you esteem Christ as greater than all that came before? Do you see Him as the true ark, the one in whom God dwells, the one through whom God blesses, the one who fulfills every promise? If you truly understand what it means that the ark has passed away, you will rejoice, for it means that the fullness of God's grace has come. No more shadows. No more waiting. Christ has come, and He is sufficient in every way.

Should Not the True Ark Be Highly Esteemed by Us?

That which is glorious ought to be highly valued, and its worth recognized according to the degree of its excellence. If this is true of earthly things, how much more of divine things? The transcendent glory of the Gospel should awaken in us a deep and lasting reverence for Christ, the true Ark. If the earthly ark, a mere shadow, was esteemed so highly by the people of God, how much more should we cherish the reality it prefigured?

This does not belittle the Ark of the Covenant, nor does it cause us to despise it. The Law was glorious, and it deserves to be honored for what it revealed—the character of God, His wisdom, His worship, His holiness, and the necessity of atonement. The ark was not given in vain. It was a most fitting revelation for the church at the time, perfectly suited to the unfolding of God's redemptive plan. Christ Himself, who is infinite wisdom, appointed it as a type to direct the thoughts of the faithful toward the true Ark, which is Himself.

Paul affirms this when he writes, "Wherefore the law was our schoolmaster to bring us unto Christ, that we might be justified by faith," (Galatians 3:24). The ark of the covenant was a type—a signpost pointing toward the fulfillment of all things in Christ. It taught the people of God to look beyond the shadow to the substance, beyond the ceremony to the reality.

So now, with the true Ark revealed, should we not esteem *Him* above all else? Should we not recognize that in Christ, the fullness of God's *covenant of faith* is made known? The ceremonial law had its time and purpose, and its Gospel messages, though veiled, was glorious in its day. But it was always meant to lead *to* Christ. To hold fast to the ark while ignoring its fulfillment would be like treasuring the schoolmaster while rejecting the lesson. The Law was given to bring us to Christ, and in Him, we find all that the ark ever signified—God's presence, His covenant, His mercy, and His redemption. If the ark was cherished, how much more should we cherish Christ?

Chapter 2: The Moral Law

"And after the second veil, the tabernacle which is called the Holiest of all; Which had the golden censer, and the ark of the covenant overlaid round about with gold, wherein was the golden pot that had manna, and Aaron's rod that budded, and the tables of the covenant; and over it the cherubims of glory shadowing the mercy seat; of which we cannot now speak particularly," (Hebrews 9:3-5).

Beyond the second curtain lay the Most Holy Place, the holiest of all, the sacred space where atonement was made and the throne of God was established. The reference to the second curtain is intentional, distinguishing it from the first, which marked the entrance to the holy place from the outer court. This second veil separated the holy place from the most holy, signifying the inaccessibility of God's presence apart from His appointed mediator. The *holiest* of all was not merely another room; it was the place of divine dwelling, where God's *throne* rested above the mercy seat.

Inside this most sacred chamber were the golden censer and the ark of the covenant, which was entirely overlaid with gold, both within and without. This ark, the central object of the Holy of Holies, was not an empty chest—it contained holy things, the symbols of God's covenant with His people: the tablets of the Law, Aaron's rod that budded, and the golden pot of manna. Each item bore testimony to God's faithfulness, authority, and provision.

Yet the writer of Hebrews draws a special connection between the altar of incense and the ark itself. According to Exodus 30:6, the altar of incense was not inside the Holy of Holies but stood in the first part of the tabernacle, just before the veil. Why, then, does Hebrews place it within the Most Holy Place? The answer lies in its *function*. On the Day of Atonement, the high priest took a censer full of burning coals from the altar and brought it *inside* the veil, where he offered incense before the mercy seat: "And he shall take a censer full of burning coals of fire from off the altar before the LORD, and his hands full of sweet incense beaten small, and bring it within the vail," (Leviticus 16:12). Though physically positioned outside, the altar of incense was intimately tied to the Holy of Holies, for its purpose was fulfilled there.

This speaks to a greater reality—the *linear pattern* of heavenly things. The tabernacle, when viewed as a blueprint laid out upon the earth, appears as a horizontal structure. But its true design stretches heavenward, like a *ladder* reaching to God. Men could not construct it as such, for they are bound to the earth, unlike the seraphim who fly before the throne. Instead, it was *spread out* across the land, marked in a way that, when perceived correctly, pointed *upward*. The Tower of Babel was man's attempt to build his own way to heaven, an act of rebellion. The tabernacle, however, was God's appointed means, structured as a pathway toward His presence. If one were to tilt their perspective, they would see it as it was meant to be—a ladder ascending to the highest place, the dwelling of God.

Each section was a threshold, leading to the next. Men passed through these spaces to draw nearer, step by step, until reaching the Most Holy Place, the chamber of God's covenant, where the ark was kept. Here, within the ark, lay the tablets of the covenant—the Decalogue, the very words of God, the testimony of His righteous standard.

This was the first and most significant of the three items kept in the ark. The high priest, entering once a year, came before the very throne of God, where His presence was most gloriously displayed above the mercy seat. Nowhere else on earth had such a revelation of divine majesty until the coming of Christ in the flesh. The veil separated this glory from the outside, shielding those in the holy place from direct exposure. Only the high priest, with incense, prayer, and the blood of atonement, could enter (Leviticus 16:9).

And here is found the mirror of God. He has a mirror that reflects His character, a revelation of His holiness and justice. This mirror, displayed in the Holy of Holies, revealed the divine attributes, if men would only look and understand. It was a *life-giving* mirror, a vision of God's righteousness, seen in part by John in his heavenly vision of Revelation and explained by the writer of Hebrews as the work of Christ, *the Great High Priest.*

This mirror does not cease. Faith and hope will one day give way to sight, but love remains. And what do the saints in glory love? They love what they now fully know— their High Priest, the Lamb who was slain, the sacrifice that perfectly satisfied the Most High. The ark and all its symbols were but types of the Christ to come.

Yet even within this ceremonial type, one of the greatest objects ever placed upon the earth was the Moral Law of God. Christ is the *embodiment* of this law. He is the ark, the living testimony of God's righteousness. He is the resurrection and the life, the fulfillment of every promise contained *in* the ark. He is the mercy seat, *crowned* as King, attended by angels, holding a ministry beyond all who came before Him.

For those in Christ, the law within the ark is no longer a weight of condemnation but a comfort, as all parts to the *covenant of faith* are. Christians, too, are placed in the ark, metaphorically, as those who *belong* to Him. Just as the Law, the manna, and the rod were sealed within, so too are believers kept in Christ, surrounded by His word, nourished by His provision, and governed by His righteous rule.

Doctrine: *The Law is a Reflection of the Attributes of God, Fulfilled in Jesus Christ*

The ark of the covenant held the Law. That may not seem like much at first glance, but pause a moment—why was the Law *inside* the ark, in the most holy place, behind the veil, sealed away from sight? It wasn't there for decoration. The Law wasn't just a list of rules; it was a reflection of God Himself. It was His character set in words, His righteousness written in stone. When God tells men to be like Him—whether in the first covenant of works in the garden or in the Covenant of Grace (or *covenant of faith*)—He is calling them to reflect His character.

The simplest way to put it is this: to emulate the Law is to emulate God. That's the whole point. If Adam was to remain holy, he had to mirror the holiness of his Creator. The Law, summed up, is this: "Do this and live." It wasn't arbitrary. It was the very structure of righteousness. If a man—Adam or anyone else—transgresses the Law, he doesn't just break a rule; he mars the image of God in himself. He walks *contrary to the nature of holiness*. He no longer reflects his Maker.

And what does that make him? A criminal. A rebel. A lawbreaker. Or, as Christ put it bluntly, "being evil" (Matthew 7:11).

That's a hard pill to swallow for people who like to think of themselves as *mostly decent*. But Jesus was clear. Imperfection is not neutrality—it's *evil*. A man who does not perfectly reflect the Moral Law is *not* good. He is, in the language of Christ, *evil*. And God, being perfect, knows that reflecting His character is the highest good for His creatures. That is why, "the law of the LORD is perfect, converting the soul," (Psalm 19:7). The Law is perfect because God is perfect. The standard is righteous because the Standard-Giver is righteous. The *1647 Westminster Confession of Faith* describes the Law as, "the perfect rule of righteousness," (19:2). That means God's righteousness is not a vague idea—it's a measurable reality.

Chapter 2: The Moral Law

What Does It Mean to Be Righteous?

If we go by the simplest definition, righteousness means upholding the Law perfectly. But that's too shallow. Biblical righteousness is more than just following rules—it's a matter of *character and conduct*. The Law isn't just something to recite; it's something to be *lived*. A righteous man doesn't merely *know* what is right; he *does* what is right. His conduct is the outward evidence of his inward state.

This is where the idea of judgment comes in. When we judge rightly, we don't do so based on our feelings or opinions; we judge by an *objective reality*—God's Moral Law. A thing is either righteous or it isn't. And the only absolute standard of righteousness is the *character of God*. To reject the Law is to reject *that* character. It's to decide that God's holiness is unnecessary and that we can come up with something better. And how many *supposed* Christians reject the Law of God today? They want to be without the Law. That's what *lawlessness* is. It's not just disobedience—it's defiance. To be "lawless" is to be destitute of the Law. And if one is destitute of the Law, he is *destitute* of the character of God.

What does Christ say to such people? "And then will I profess unto them, I never knew you: depart from me, ye that *work iniquity*," (Matthew 7:23). These are not Old Testament words—they are New Testament words, spoken by Christ Himself. And what is His charge against them? *Lawlessness*. Law-*less*. They rejected the Law, which means they rejected the God who gave it. They would not reflect His righteousness, and so they *are cast out*.

Only those who uphold the Law—who reflect the character of God—are accepted by Him. And where is the Law kept? Not on a mountaintop. Not in the public square. It is sealed away in the Most Holy Place, inside the ark, hidden behind the veil. It is the treasure of the sanctuary, the heart of true worship.

Who Upholds the Law?

If righteousness is measured by how well a man reflects God's character, then who succeeds? Who does this perfectly? The answer is simple—no one but Christ. And yet, the Law still stands. It still binds. The *1647 Westminster Larger Catechism* asks, "What is the moral law?" and answers:

> "The moral law is the declaration of the will of God to mankind, directing and binding everyone to personal, perfect, and perpetual conformity and obedience thereunto, in the frame and disposition of the whole man, soul and body, and in performance of all those duties of holiness and righteousness which he oweth to God and man: promising life upon the fulfilling, and threatening death upon the breach of it," (Deuteronomy 5:1-3, 31, 33; Luke 10:26-27; Galatians 3:10; 1 Thessalonians 5:23; Luke 1:75; Acts 14:16; Romans 10:5; Galatians 3:10, 12).

The Law demands absolute, *unflinching* obedience. There is no gray area. To uphold it is life; to break it is death. And this is not because God is arbitrary, but because perfection is the only acceptable standard. "Be ye therefore perfect, even as your Father which is in heaven is perfect," (Matthew 5:48). Who said *that*? The Greek emphasis here is *by way of consequence*—because God is perfect, you must be perfect. There's no negotiating.

God acts perfectly, therefore His children should act perfectly. Paul puts it simply: "Be ye therefore followers of God, as dear children," (Ephesians 5:1). *Followers* of God must *imitate* Him. And what is there to imitate? His character. His righteousness. His Moral Law.

Paul drives the point home: "And walk in love, as Christ also hath loved us, and hath given himself for us an offering and a sacrifice to God for a sweet-smelling savour," (Ephesians 5:2). The language here is unmistakably drawn from Old Testament sacrifice. The Law was not cast aside—it was fulfilled in Christ. And the difference between those who belong to Christ and those who do not is simple: the *lawless* reject the Law, while the *righteous* uphold it.

Paul clarifies: "For this ye know, that no whoremonger, nor unclean person, nor covetous man, who is an idolater, hath any inheritance in the kingdom of Christ and of God," (Ephesians 5:5). There is no room for lawlessness in the Kingdom. The distinction is stark—those who reject the Moral Law live in wickedness; those who uphold it walk in love, in righteousness, in holiness.

And what does John say of the saints in glory? "We shall be like him," (1 John 3:2). That is the final fulfillment of the Law—to reflect the attributes of God in perfect obedience. The prayer of Christ is this: "Thy will be done in earth, as it is in heaven," (Matthew 6:10). In heaven, the Law is obeyed. There is no rebellion, no sin, no deviation from righteousness. The will of God is fulfilled in every respect.

The Law remains at the center, just as it sat at the center of the ark, in the heart of the tabernacle, in the Most Holy Place. And upon that ark sits Christ, the King, the perfect fulfillment of the Law. He is the embodiment of God's righteousness, the fulfillment of the covenant, and the only one who has ever perfectly kept the Law.

To reject the Law is to reject Him. To cherish the Law is to cherish Him. The Law is not burdensome—it is life, for it leads to Christ, in whom all righteousness is fulfilled. And in Him, the glory of God is perfectly revealed.

The Law as Understood as the Objective Nature of God

If a man does not understand the Law as the reflection of God's character, he will misunderstand *everything*—Adam's failure, Christ's success, the covenants of God, and the way of salvation. The Law is not some set of arbitrary rules; it is the very essence of what it means to be *holy*, because it is a direct expression of God's nature. This is why it sits at the *center* of the ark, behind the veil, in the most sacred place on earth. It is not just a list of commands—it is the testimony of God's attributes.

This is the foundation of the covenants. God makes covenants with His Son and with men, and at the heart of every covenant is the Law. The ark of the covenant holds the tablets of the covenant, because Christ—the true Ark—upholds the Law perfectly. He does not break it, He does not bend it, He does not abolish it. He fulfills it.

What is a Covenant? A covenant is God's way of saving sinners. Get the *covenant* wrong, and you get *everything* wrong. The whole history of redemption is a story of covenants. It answers the one question that matters most since the fall: *How can a sinful man approach a holy God?*

Mankind, left to himself, is lost. The fall has plunged him into ruin, into what the *1647 Westminster Larger Catechism* calls, "an estate of sin and misery" (Q. 23). The fall didn't just make life difficult—it made holiness impossible. Sinful man cannot survive in the presence of a holy God, much less draw near to Him. Every time God manifests His holiness in creation, it is met with fear and trembling.

When God appeared to Moses in the burning bush, what did He say? "Draw not nigh hither: put off thy shoes from off thy feet, for the place whereon thou standest is holy ground," (Exodus 3:5). Moses had to strip away even his sandals before stepping forward. Why? Because when God's holiness intersects with creation, men must react in a specific way. It is not up for negotiation. And yet, how many people in how many churches through how many ages *feel* their way through their worship? What does a holy God think of all that?

God has not chosen to intersect with every man through a burning bush. Instead, He has made Himself known through *covenant*. The ark of the *covenant*, housing the tablets of the *covenant*, points to this reality—it sits in the Holy of Holies where Christ, the fulfillment of the *covenant*, reigns in glory.

Covenant is God's node of relating to men. The 1647 *Westminster Larger Catechism* puts it plainly: *"God does not leave all men to perish in the estate of sin and misery, into which they fell by the breach of the first covenant, commonly called the Covenant of Works; but of his mere love and mercy delivers his elect out of it, and brings them into an estate of salvation by the second covenant, commonly called the Covenant of Grace."* (1 Thess. 5:9; Gal. 3:10, 12; Titus 3:4–7; Gal. 3:21; Rom. 3:20–22).

If covenant is the *only* way of salvation, then *twisting* the nature of covenant is a dangerous thing. This is why men must not hold the ark in disdain. They must not despise the tablets of the covenant, or the Law they contain. Yet many do. They recoil at the idea of God's Law, treating it as though it were the enemy of grace. But what does Christ say? *"Whoever therefore breaks one of the least of these commandments, and teaches men so, shall be called least in the kingdom of heaven,"* (Matthew 5:19). To dismiss the Law is to dismiss the very nature of God. And there are *eternal consequences* for that.

In Hebrew, the word for covenant is *berith*. It means "to cut a covenant." Cutting implies *sacrifice*. A covenant (generally speaking) is not a light agreement—it is sealed in blood. When a covenant is made, an oath is sworn, and death is the consequence of breaking it.

In Genesis 15:10, when God made a covenant with Abram, He had him cut animals in half and lay them opposite each other. Then God Himself passed between them. What was the message? *Let it be done to Me as it was done to these animals if I fail to keep My word.* The Greek equivalent of *berith* is *diathēkē*, meaning both "covenant" and "testament." This is why Scripture speaks of Christ as the Mediator of a *New Testament*. It is a *new covenant*, sealed with His own blood, a new *testament* to the covenant of faith.

Every salvation covenant contains three key elements:
1. A promise of eternal life.
2. The conditions required to obtain the promise.
3. A punitive sanction for breaking the covenant.

A covenant is not a casual agreement—it is binding. And because God is holy, *every* covenant requires holiness. Every covenant demands *complete* sanctification. This is why the ark holds the Moral Law, and why it is *covered* by the mercy seat. The Law requires *perfection*. The mercy seat provides atonement for those who have broken it.

If a man does not uphold his end of the covenant, he is judged. And here's the key—he does not get to decide whether or not to participate in the covenant. He is *born* into it. God does not give men the option to "opt out." Every man is in covenant with God, whether he wants to be or not. He is either under the Covenant of Works (by conception), in

Adam, bound to the Law and its curse... Or he is under the Covenant of Grace (in being born again), in Christ, bound to the Law and its fulfillment. There is no third option. There are only two Covenants. All men are in covenant with God, but there are *only* two covenants that define their standing before Him.

1. **The Covenant of Works** – Given to Adam in the garden. This covenant is simple: *Do this and live.* It required perfect obedience to the Law, and Adam failed. His failure plunged all of humanity into sin and death.
2. **The Covenant of Grace (or Faith)** – Instituted after the fall, this covenant also requires perfect obedience to the Law. But it is no longer Adam, or any other man, who must keep it. Christ, the second Adam, fulfills it on behalf of His people. His obedience is counted as theirs. His righteousness is given to them. And in Him, they receive eternal life.

The covenant did not change. The requirements did not change. Only the *Mediator* changed. Adam failed. Christ succeeded.

There is no happiness apart from the Law of God. That statement is as true today as it was the day God inscribed the commandments on stone. The world scoffs at this idea, insisting that freedom from the Law is the key to happiness. But what does Scripture say? *"Blessed is the man that walketh not in the counsel of the ungodly, nor standeth in the way of sinners, nor sitteth in the seat of the scornful. But his delight is in the law of the LORD; and in his law doth he meditate day and night,"* (Psalm 1:1-2). Happiness is not found in rebellion. It is found in conformity to God's character. That is why covenant is *essential*. Covenant is the mode by which God's Law is upheld. It is the structure through which righteousness is made known. And it is the only way for man to be made whole. A man cannot find peace outside the covenant. He cannot find joy outside the Law. And he cannot find life outside Christ. To reject the covenant is to reject life itself.

The Law in the Ark of the Covenant and Christ's Fulfillment

The Law is no mere collection of rules; it is the *summary* of all duty, the guide to all righteousness, and the very reflection of God's holy character. And in His wisdom, God took that Law and placed it in the ark of His covenant, in the holiest place, beneath the mercy seat. This was no accident. The Moral Law is central, unmovable, the foundation of all righteousness. The Law is the rule and guide for all of life. Everything that a man must do, everything required for eternal life, is contained in the Ten Commandments. It is the great summary of all moral duty. Christ Himself confirmed this when He said: *"Thou shalt love the Lord thy God with all thy heart, and with all thy soul, and with all thy mind. This is the first and great commandment. And the second is like unto it, Thou shalt love thy neighbour as thyself,"* (Matthew 22:37-39). This is the essence of all righteousness. The whole of the Christian life is bound up in these words. To love God is to obey Him. To love one's neighbor is to reflect God's righteousness. Everything that pleases God, every act of devotion, every duty of obedience, is summed up in these commands. And these commands were not invented at Sinai; they were *simply written down there*.

Christ and the Law at Sinai

The Moral Law of Sinai is not separate from the Gospel. It is *part* of the covenant of grace. Christ, the eternal King, was the one who gave the Law to Moses. He was the voice from the mountain, the Lawgiver of Israel, and He is still the Lawgiver of the New Covenant.

To separate the Law *from* the Gospel is to *misunderstand* both (which is typical today). The Gospel does not abolish the Law; it *fulfills* it. This is why those who belong to Christ are, in a spiritual sense, placed inside the ark *with* the Law. They are wrapped up in Christ, hidden in Him, and there, beside the tablets of the covenant, they find their security. They cannot escape the Law. They cannot avoid it. They cannot reject it. For they are bound up in the Ark with it. And just as the mercy seat covered the Law in the ark, so Christ's blood covers the believer. But the Law remains, holy and unbroken, a testimony to God's eternal righteousness. To disregard the Law, then, is to *disregard* Christ. To trample the commandments underfoot is to trample the Son of God underfoot. This is why the Law is called *the Law of Christ*: *"Bear ye one another's burdens, and so fulfil the law of Christ,"* (Galatians 6:2). This is no minor matter. To despise the Law is to despise *the Gospel itself*. The writer of Hebrews spends great effort to show that Christ fulfills all that the types and shadows of the Old Covenant pointed toward. He is *the* Ark. He is the faithful High Priest. He is the Law made flesh, the Bread of Heaven, the Rod of divine authority. And because of this, the obligations of the Law are not abolished—they are heightened.

There is nothing in the Ten Commandments that was required of Moses that is not required of the Christian today. The *standard* has not changed. The Moral Law still demands perfection. And while no man can attain this perfection, Christ, in fulfilling the Law, grants His Spirit in greater measure to enable obedience. Moses knew this. Yet many Christians today seem to have forgotten this. They speak of grace as if it were a license to ignore God's commands, as if obedience were some burden too great for New Testament believers to bear. But what does Christ say? *"For my yoke is easy, and my burden is light,"* (Matthew 11:30). What does John say? *"For this is the love of God, that we keep his commandments: and his commandments are not grievous,"* (1 John 5:3). The Law is not a burden. It is not a *hindrance* to grace. It is the *very expression* of God's will for His people. And Christ, rather than diminishing its requirements, magnified them. He did not come to dissolve the Law but to fulfill it. *"Think not that I am come to destroy the law, or the prophets: I am not come to destroy, but to fulfil. For verily I say unto you, Till heaven and earth pass, one jot or one tittle shall in no wise pass from the law, till all be fulfilled,"* (Matthew 5:17-18). What Christ fulfilled is *still* in effect. He did not remove one commandment. He did not lower the standard. If anything, *He raised it.*

The Law in the Life of the Believer

One does not hear about the ark of the covenant anymore because *Christ is the Ark.* The ark itself is no longer needed because the *fulfillment* of the ark's *type* has come. But the realities that surrounded the ark remain as important as ever. The Law still sits beneath the throne of God. John saw the ark in heaven, because it represents Christ's rule, His kingdom, and His perfect Law.

This is why the Moral Law is still in force today. It was in force before Sinai. It was in force at Sinai. And it is in force today in the kingdom of Christ.

To be a believer is to obey Christ. Faith and obedience cannot be separated. The one proves the other. James makes this plain: *"But wilt thou know, O vain man, that faith without works is dead?"* (James 2:20). Faith is not mere belief. It is reliance, trust, and obedience. True faith is faith that works. And that work is obedience to God's commands. Obedience does not earn salvation. It is not a condition of entering into the ark of Christ. But it is the *evidence* of being inside. This is why Christ says: *"If ye keep my commandments, ye shall abide in my love; even as I have kept my Father's commandments, and abide in his love,"* (John 15:10). And this is why Paul says:

"Do we then make void the law through faith? God forbid: yea, we establish the law," (Romans 3:31). Faith does not abolish the Law. It upholds it. It makes obedience possible. It is the evidence of true salvation. The Law remains. It sits at the heart of the covenant, beneath the mercy seat, in the throne room of heaven. It is the rule of life, the guide to holiness, the standard of righteousness. It cannot be discarded, ignored, or diminished. To be in Christ is to be placed in the ark beside the Law. To be covered by His mercy is to be joined to His commandments. There is no separation between grace and obedience. This is why Christ said: *"Not every one that saith unto me, Lord, Lord, shall enter into the kingdom of heaven; but he that doeth the will of my Father which is in heaven,"* (Matthew 7:21). The Law is still the standard. Christ has fulfilled it, but He has not erased it. He has made it clearer, more binding, more glorious. The only question is whether we will obey it.

The Law and the Gospel: The Fulfillment of the Ark's Testimony

The Law stands firm, unyielding, a mirror to the soul of every man who dares to look into it. It is a reflection of God's own character, set down in ten immutable words, preserved in stone, locked within the Ark of the Covenant, and surrounded by the holiness of the Most High. It forbids all sin, commands all righteousness, and stands as the great and terrible witness against every transgression.

The Law and the Ark: Held Secure in Christ

The Law remains *in* the Ark. It is not abolished, not set aside, not hidden away, but rather *encased* within the very throne of God. And over it sits the mercy seat, where the blood of atonement is sprinkled, where justice and grace meet, where the righteous standard and the satisfaction of that standard embrace.

The Christian lives in the shadow of this great reality. He does not wander far from the Law, nor does he shun it. No, he is bound up in Christ, and Christ is bound up in the covenant. And there, nestled within the Ark of His righteousness, the believer finds the tablets of the Law resting alongside him. What does this mean? It means that the Law is not an enemy to the Christian. It is not some distant relic of a bygone era, to be cast aside with the broken tablets of Sinai. No, it is his guide, his tutor, his rule of life. It shows him his sin, presses him to humility, and drives him to the mercy seat above it. *"For I delight in the Law of God after the inward man,"* (Romans 7:22).

The Law Searches the Heart

The Law does not merely ask for outward obedience—it demands the obedience of the heart, the soul, and the mind. Moses knew this well: *"If thou seek him with all thy heart and with all thy soul,"* (Deuteronomy 4:29). Jesus confirmed it: *"Thou shalt love the Lord thy God with all thy heart, and with all thy soul, and with all thy mind,"* (Matthew 22:37-38). Not some of the heart. Not a fraction of the soul. Not an occasional devotion of the mind. *All.* This is why the believer cannot be content with external righteousness, with a mere profession of faith, with a hollow religion that nods at grace but sneers at holiness. The Law presses *deeper*. It searches out hypocrisy, exposes hidden sin, and demands that the whole man be conformed to the character of God. But here is the glory of it: the *believer* is not left *to his own strength*. The Law commands perfection, but Christ gives the power to pursue it. It is the Spirit of Christ who enables obedience, who bends the will, who fills the soul with a love for righteousness.

The Law and the Mercy Seat: The Picture of Redemption

Picture the scene: The Holy of Holies. The Ark at its center. Above it, the shekinah glory of God, dwelling between the cherubim, where the blood of the covenant is sprinkled, the blood that satisfies the wrath of the Almighty. Inside the Ark, three things: The tablets of the Law—God's righteous standard. The golden pot of manna—God's provision. Aaron's rod that budded—God's authority to bring life from death. And within this scene, the Christian finds himself, hidden in Christ, preserved in the Ark, surrounded by the holiness of God. What does *this* mean? It means that the Law still stands, still accuses, still demands. It means that righteousness is still required. It means that sin is still judged. But it also means that grace is provided. That atonement is made. That mercy reigns.

The Law as a Mirror and a Guide

To the redeemed, the Law serves as a mirror. It shows them their sin, their need, their utter inability to stand before God apart from Christ. *"Let no man deceive you; he that committeth sin is of the devil,"* (1 John 3:7). But to those in Christ, it also *serves as a guide*. It is the *rule* by which they *walk*, the standard by which they measure holiness, the reflection of the God they love and long to be like. *"And because God is the great King, and our God and Redeemer, Christians are bound to keep his Ten Commandments showing forth life and godliness; keeping the commandments shows saving faith, without which people are just talk."* Faith without works is dead. A profession without obedience is empty. To claim Christ and yet spurn His Law is to walk in darkness. The true believer is in Christ, wrapped in His righteousness, nestled within the Ark of His covenant. And in that Ark, beside the Law, he abides. The Law is not cast away. It is upheld. *"But as he which hath called you is holy, so be ye holy in all manner of conversation; Because it is written, Be ye holy; for I am holy,"* (1 Peter 1:15-16). Peter does not conjure some new teaching here. He reaches back to the Law, to Leviticus, to the commands of the holy God. *"Therefore shall ye observe all my statutes, and all my judgments, and do them: I am the LORD,"* (Leviticus 19:37).

The Law and the Gospel: The Complete Christian Religion

Many try to divide the two, as though Law and Gospel were at *odds*, as though grace nullifies righteousness, as though faith and obedience were rival doctrines. But the Christian religion is not divided. It is one. The Moral Law and the Gospel are not enemies. They are companions. The one demands, the other provides. The one exposes sin, the other cleanses it. The one commands holiness, the other grants the power to attain it. *"Fulfil the Law of Christ,"* (Galatians 6:2). This is why the believer does not live by vague religious sentiment, by mere feelings of persuasion, but by the clear commands of the holy God. He does not rest in general notions of divine love—he walks in the very Laws of the King who rules from the Ark of His covenant. And what does he find there? The very nature and essence of God Himself.

The Law's Ultimate Purpose

What is required of believers? The Law tells them. *"Do this and thou shalt live."* What does the Moral Law reveal? The depth of man's fall, his inability to meet its standard, the inevitable condemnation of every sinner outside of Christ. *"Thou shalt die."* But what does the Gospel declare? *"Behold the Lamb of God, which taketh away the sin of the world!"* This is why the Ark was *covered* with the mercy seat. This is why the Law, though firm and unrelenting, was hidden beneath the blood of atonement. This is why, in the vision of the heavenly temple, John sees the Ark, not as a relic of the past, but as the very throne of the reigning Christ. The Law stands. The Gospel prevails. And together, they testify of the holiness, the justice, and the grace of God. *"Wherefore the law is holy, and the commandment holy, and just, and good,"* (Romans 7:12).

The believer does not fear the Law. He delights in it. For he is in Christ. And in Christ, he is in the Ark. And in the Ark, beneath the mercy seat, beside the tablets of the covenant, he is safe—safe in the righteousness of the King who rules from heaven, whose throne is justice, whose footstool is mercy, and whose kingdom is everlasting. His obedience was not a halfway measure, nor a temporary fix, but a complete and perfect fulfillment of the law on behalf of his people. The righteous requirement of the law was not set aside but fully upheld in Christ. The Father, in his infinite wisdom, did not overlook justice, but he *satisfied* it in the work of his Son. It is for this reason that believers can stand before a holy God, not in their own righteousness, but clothed in the merit of Christ, secured under the mercy seat, resting in the ark of his covenant.

But consider what this means for you. If you are in Christ, your position before God is one of security and favor, not because of anything you have done, but because you are covered by the very righteousness of Christ. The Law, which once condemned, is now the very thing that demonstrates your safety—because it has been perfectly fulfilled for you. The tablets remain in the ark, not to accuse you, but as a testament to the completed work of the Redeemer. The Law no longer stands over you as a judge, but rather as a guide, directing your steps in love and obedience.

Does this mean that Christians are *free to live as they please*, with no regard for the commandments of God? Quite the opposite. If Christ went to such great lengths to uphold the Law, should not his people desire to reflect that same Law in their lives? The Law is not the means of salvation, but *it is the outward mark* of those who have been saved. It is the *pattern of holiness*, the shape of righteousness, the very character of God expressed in precept and principle. And since the Spirit of Christ dwells within his people, conforming them to his likeness, obedience is not a burden but a delight.

Yet, even in our obedience, we find ourselves weak, stumbling, falling short of the perfection that the Law demands. This should not lead to despair, but to greater reliance on Christ. The Law remains, the tablets of the covenant still rest *in* the ark, but so too does the mercy seat remain upon it. The Law is there, but so is the blood of the sacrifice. The Christian is bound to holiness, but he is also bound to mercy. And that mercy, flowing from the throne of grace, enables the believer to walk in the path of righteousness—not to earn salvation, but to reflect the salvation that has already been given.

So then, how should one respond to such a glorious truth? With gratitude, with reverence, and with a heart devoted to the service of the King who sits enthroned above the mercy seat. You are not outside the covenant, wandering in the wilderness without a guide. You are not under the condemnation of the Law, crushed beneath its weight with no hope of escape (as Adam felt for a time after his sin). No, you are in the ark, carried by Christ, preserved by his merit, and sustained by his grace. The Law, once a terror, is now a tutor; once a burden, now a blessing. You are in Christ, and in him, the demands of righteousness are satisfied, and the way of holiness is made clear. What more could be required than to walk in the light of that truth, striving, by the Spirit's power, to reflect the character of the One who has loved you and given himself for you?

His deity enabled his obedience to be of inestimable value to you on behalf of the Father. Your sins, which are infinite against an infinite God, need an infinite sacrifice; and you know it. Christ's deity enabled him to offer such a sacrifice of inestimable worth for you personally. His humanity enabled him to obey in your place. Truly, as Hebrews says, the blood of bulls and goats cannot save; rather, it must be a human sacrifice for sin that atones for the sins of humans (Hebrews 10:4). However, even though Christ's sacrifice was infinite, and infinitely expiated and propitiated sin and wrath, the obedience of Christ does not abrogate your responsibility to show forth your salvation by obedience to that moral code of God's holy character.

Many times, people use the "righteousness of Christ" as a means to sin—no more law. Shall we go on sinning that grace may abound? Certainly not. Paul's words should ring in the ears of every believer. There are two uses of the law for you to consider being in the ark of God and under the sprinkled blood of atonement, laying with the tablets of the covenant, so to speak. The Law as the duty of the creature to his Creator and the Law as a means of acquiring eternal life. Christ fulfilled the second use, whereas the first continues to be binding on *all* men. Men must be holy, which means they must reflect the character of God's holiness. This is the difficult road that sanctification takes the church. "By the which will we are sanctified through the offering of the body of Jesus Christ once for all," (Heb. 10:10). The phrase "by the which" is the Law, the will of God. "But we know that the law is good, if a man use it lawfully," (1 Tim. 1:8).

The use of the Law is a representation of virtue, goodness, and holiness because it is a mirror of *God*. Imagine if you were to lay upon a large mirror that would engulf your whole person. It was 100 feet by 100 feet, and you lay on top of it right in the middle, that wherever you looked, it reflected your whole being back to you. And yet, let's say it is a special mirror that reflected back to you your person, redeemed as it is in Christ, still imperfect. You see its deformities, and it showed and reflected back all your imperfections. It might be hard to see all of them at once, but you would quickly get the picture that the mirror showed all your deformities, even as redeemed. Now consider that such a mirror is the Law, and it shows all your deformities. You see pieces of it here and there, and depth changes, and degrees heighten day by day. It is the way in which you can have glorious communion with God by obeying it in degrees to go on to perfection (Leviticus 18:5; Romans 7:10).

It is, though, impossible to keep because of the fall, and you know it, which is why you are happy to be *in* the ark of his covenant. But it is still a command of God binding you to it. The Law acts as a mirror to show us who we are before God (James 1:23). It demonstrates the curse against man (Romans 3:19), and it is also used to deter him from sinful actions (to restrain him from it – 1 Timothy 1:9). It is the tool by which Christ uses to bring sinners to himself. Romans 10:4 shows us that the end of the road of the Law is Christ, "Christ is the end of the law for righteousness to everyone that believeth."

The Law is used to show us what Christ had to do on our behalf. It shows us how to be perfect as he was perfect. It shows us how far we have to go to be perfect to follow his pattern. Such a law is called a covenant (Exodus 34:28; Deuteronomy 5:2; 4:13; 9:9).

Consider this finally; *this* is very important. The Mosaic covenant, where the Law was formally delivered by the messenger of the covenant, the Christ, on Sinai, was not formally and merely just the Gospel in the covenant of grace, but that which was more *mingled* with ceremony and types, in shadows. In the clear light of day by Christ, the Covenant of Grace requires not only obedience but also promises and strength by the Holy Spirit to obey it. Clear light in promises and by strength *do not* clearly appear at Sinai when the Law was given, as is seen in the difference between the administration of the Mosaic Covenant and New Covenant in Genesis 3:15 and Jeremiah 31:31–34. That is why the ark of the covenant is a type of the Christ to come—Christ who would fulfill such things perfectly for his people.

Chapter 2: The Moral Law

This does not mean that the godly at the time of Moses did not have the strength to obey God's Law, but only that this strength did not come from the *Mosaic* testament, but only by Christ and the Spirit, which was shrouded in types and shadows in that Mosaic testament; Christ to come looked on by faith. You look on Christ; they looked on Christ through the ark. You look to see Christ as the ark, and you understand the ark and its covenant testimony as that which Christ secures you in and by. The Mosaic Covenant and the Covenant of Grace are superimposed on one another in this way, they are one and the same thing in sum and substance. Just their administration and testator were different. This is where the Law is republished to a certain extent to demonstrate sin, and that the Messiah in the full-orbed Covenant of Grace secures the believer's salvation by his work.

The 1647 Westminster Confession says of this in 7:5, "This covenant was differently administered in the time of the law and in the time of the Gospel: under the law it was administered by promises, prophecies, sacrifices, circumcision, the paschal lamb, and other types and ordinances delivered to the people of the Jews, all fore-signifying Christ to come, which were for that time sufficient and efficacious, through the operation of the Spirit, to instruct and build up the elect in faith in the promised Messiah, by whom they had full remission of sins and eternal salvation; and is called the Old Testament."

The law you are to love is the same as it has always been because Jesus Christ is the same *yesterday, today,* and *forever*, because God is the author of his own character. Do you believe that? Is he the same yesterday? Or is that just a bible verse you gloss over? He requires us to be like him and obey it. He added special motives for obedience for his church in ceremonies and types and shadows in the Old Testament, which Christ fulfilled, though this does not abrogate the moral law for Gentiles. Keep in mind that there is only one church, one kingdom, one King, and one law, which remains binding on everyone (Ephesians 2:14; Romans 11:17). The manner in which the moral Law was initially proclaimed and published implies its universality to all people for all time. That is why, in such a gracious covenant as the ark was part of, the tablets of the law were found within it—within Christ. The New Testament confirms its *binding* nature. Matthew 5:17, Jesus says, "Think not that I am come to destroy the law, or the prophets: I am not come to destroy, but to fulfill." He does not do away with it. He fulfills it. (*cf.* Romans 13:9; James 2:8–11; Ephesians 6:2). Only God can abrogate his law, and he has not done so, for it is impossible since it shows his *character*. Instead, he has given you a picture of his character in the ark, where you reside in Christ; holiness under the mercy seat in and by his law, fulfilled by Christ's mediation. The Law is a reflection of the attributes of God, fulfilled in Jesus Christ; and do you not wish to be like Christ, for God's glory? "O how love I thy law! it is my meditation all the day," (Psa. 119:97).

Chapter 3: The Manna

"And after the second veil, the tabernacle which is called the Holiest of all; Which had the golden censer, and the ark of the covenant overlaid round about with gold, wherein was the golden pot that had manna, and Aaron's rod that budded, and the tables of the covenant; and over it the cherubims of glory shadowing the mercyseat; of which we cannot now speak particularly," (Heb. 9:3-5).

After the second curtain, there was the tabernacle called the holy things of holy things. The sense being after entering behind the second curtain, the veil, referring to the curtain which separated the holy place from the most holy place, it is called the second curtain to distinguish it from the curtain at the entrance to the holy place from the outside court. This was the Ἅγια Ἁγίων, the holy things of holy things, the Most Holy Place, the holiest of all, the place of atonement.

In the holy of holies was found the ark of the covenant, covered with gold, as a *crown* is. The holy of holies contained the ark, that covenant box, that sacred chest, which was covered around on all sides with gold, inside and outside. It contained a witness of God's character. In relation to the ark of the covenant are mentioned the tablets of the law, Aaron's rod, and the golden pot filled with manna. It is here that some ambiguity is set in this, in that, whether the rod and manna were set in the ark, or just the tablets were in the ark, and the rod and the golden pot were by the side of the ark in the shadows of the ark, is immaterial really. The Greek text is only ambiguous because the word "en" means "in" or can mean "by." But regardless of whether they are in or by, this does not negate their importance and the typology which extends from their importance, nor their place as the furniture of the holy of holies. For that reason, I will remark on them as that they, by the Spirit's direction in Hebrews, that, as the tablets were in the ark, so the golden pot and rod were there too. If the law was "en," so I conclude that the rod and pot were "en" the ark.[4]

In *this* way, the ark contained three things: the tables of the Law, Aaron's rod that budded, and the golden pot of manna. These are holy things contained in the holy ark, set in the holy of holies, in which the holy mercy seat covered and over which all the holiness of God hovered in Shekinah or holy glory.

The manna was set in the golden pot and placed in the ark of the covenant. The manna is augmented and enlarged by the mentioning of the golden pot. "And Moses said unto Aaron, Take a pot, and put an omer full of manna therein, and lay it up before the LORD, to be kept for your generations," (Exodus 16:33). Make note on this Scripture in Hebrews that the quality of the pot was gold. In it was a measure of the manna, an *omer*. It was to be set before the Lord. It was to be kept for generations.

This manna was a provision provided to the church in the time of their distress, in wandering in the wilderness

---

[4] As I said earlier, this is a point of contention in some ways.

of the world, by God, who gave them angel's food. Bread given from heaven by the ministry of angels—"Man did eat angels' food," (Psalm 78:25). This was a physical manna which turns to be considered as typical, by way of type.

Manna signifies a part, portion, or gift, prepared by God for the good of his people. Some see the word as used signifying "to distribute," and therefore it signifies a distributive gift, or food fallen from heaven to all his people.

Doctrine: *Jesus Christ is the hidden manna, the lively bread, given for the good of his covenant people.*

In the ark was manna. That's what the text says, and that's what we have to reckon with. Manna, meaning in Hebrew, "what is it?" which is a fair enough question, considering the people who first saw it had never seen anything like it before. There it was, scattered across the ground in the morning like frost, white and small, round as coriander seed, and sweet to the taste. But its meaning ran deeper than just a question of daily bread. Manna had the connotation of a provided portion—something given, something set aside, something measured out.

God gave it to them in Exodus 16:15. It wasn't something they worked for, or something they deserved. It wasn't cultivated, nor did they earn it. It was simply *given*. And yet, even as it fell from heaven, they had to gather it. Here was a mystery and a blessing wrapped up together— food from heaven, and yet it required their effort to take and eat. The people were bewildered at first, staring at it and asking, "What is it?" But God's answer was simple: "This is the bread which the Lord hath given you to eat: and withal the Lord said hereupon, ye shall know that I am the Lord your God," (Exodus 16:12, 15).

The people were in the wilderness, and hunger was beginning to gnaw at them. They had no crops, no storehouses, no means of sustaining themselves in that barren land. It would have been utter ruin if God had not intervened. He had brought them out of Egypt, and he would not leave them to starve. So, he provided. The bread came down from heaven itself—angel's food, as the psalmist calls it: "Then said the LORD unto Moses, Behold, I will rain bread from heaven for you," (Exodus 16:4). "And had rained down manna upon them to eat, and had given them of the corn of heaven," (Psalm 78:24). Here was provision from the throne of God itself, from his mercy seat, from the very government of heaven, where he ruled as King over his people.

What did it look like? It was small, round, and white, like frost on the ground. It had the appearance of coriander seed, glistening in the morning sun, and it tasted like wafers made with honey. Some said it tasted like fresh oil (Exodus 16:14, 31; Numbers 11:8). It was pleasant, sweet, enjoyable. Not a single person turned their nose up at it. It wasn't like earthly food, where one man delights in a dish and another can hardly choke it down. No, this was different. It was universally good, universally satisfying. God gave them food from heaven, and *no one* complained about the taste.

And how was it given? It cost them nothing. It rained down freely. But it came in a particular manner. It was sent with dew, carried by the night mist, and when the dew evaporated in the morning, the manna was left behind, waiting for them. They had to gather it—no one could simply sit in their tents and wait for it to appear in their bowls. It was theirs, but they had to take hold of it. And it was given only to them. No other nation woke up to find manna outside their tents. No Philistine, no Moabite, no Jebusite, no foreign people rose in the morning to a miraculous meal. It was God's food for God's people alone.

But there was a rule: gather only what you need. No hoarding, no greed, no taking more than necessary. Every man gathered for his household, just as God commanded (Exodus 16:16). If they left it lying out, it melted under the heat of the sun. If they tried to keep it overnight, thinking to store up for themselves instead of trusting in God's daily provision, it rotted and bred worms (Exodus 16:20).

And yet, a portion of it did not rot. A portion was set aside in a golden pot and placed in the ark of the covenant. A measure of that same bread, which would spoil if hoarded, was preserved by God's decree. It was to be a testimony, a witness to future generations. Not that they would *ever* see it. The manna was hidden away, deep within the holy of holies, beneath the mercy seat, in a place where no man could go except the high priest, and even then, only once a year. And even he would not have seen it, for the lid of the ark was never removed. Yet, it stood as a sacred testimony to the people. It was a reminder of God's provision, a supernatural work done for them.

Imagine the *faith* it would have taken to believe in something you had never seen (*i.e. a covenant of faith*). To know that, inside the ark, in the most holy place, under the shadow of the cherubim, there lay a golden pot filled with food from heaven itself. To trust that, though hidden, it was real. It was no different than trusting in the unseen God who had fed them in the wilderness. They had seen his provision once, and they had to believe in it still.

This manna, this mysterious bread, was more than just sustenance for the body. It was a shadow, a type, a symbol of something greater—something that would be revealed in full when the true bread from heaven came down, not to be gathered from the ground, but to be received by faith.

Christ is the manna, the true bread, the living bread from heaven, the fulfillment of the type given in the wilderness. He himself declares it plainly: "Verily, verily, I say unto you, Moses gave you not that bread from heaven; but my Father giveth you the true bread from heaven," (John 6:32). The world, in its fallen nature, is a barren wilderness—desolate, lifeless, void of true spiritual sustenance. No matter how men labor, they cannot produce the food their souls need. They are starving and do not even know it. But God, in his mercy, has provided for his people. He has sent bread from heaven, not like the manna in the wilderness that perished with the day, but true and everlasting food.

This bread came from heaven, from the very throne of God, from where the Son reigns in glory. Just as the manna rained down in Moses' time, Christ descended from heaven, not merely as another provision, but as the fulfillment of all provision. The manna in the wilderness was but a shadow; Christ is the substance. "For the bread of God is he which cometh down from heaven, and giveth life unto the world," (John 6:33, 51). He is "the Lord from heaven," (1 Cor. 15:47), the true God who took on flesh and dwelt among men. He came as the real heavenly food, far more to be esteemed than the hidden manna tucked away in the ark. That manna was concealed; Christ is revealed. That manna was given for a time; Christ is given forever.

And how did he come? He made himself of no reputation. He took upon him the form of a servant. He became poor for the sake of his people. "But made himself of no reputation, and took upon him the form of a servant, and was made in the likeness of men," (Phil. 2:7). "For ye know the grace of our Lord Jesus Christ, that, though he was rich, yet for your sakes he became poor, that ye through his poverty might be rich," (2 Cor. 8:9). The fullness of the Godhead dwelled in him bodily, and yet, he humbled himself to be the food of his people.

Even the *appearance* of the manna spoke of Christ. It was white, pure, unstained—just as he is: "For such an high priest became us, who is holy, harmless, undefiled, separate from sinners, and made higher than the heavens," (Heb. 7:26). "My beloved is white and ruddy, the chiefest among ten thousand," (Song 5:10). White for his divinity, ruddy for his humanity. Just as the Shulamite woman, though darkened by sin, was still comely in the eyes of her

Redeemer, so the Savior stands before her, shining in purity, ready to cleanse and restore.

And what of its taste? The manna was sweet, like wafers made with honey. It was delightful, satisfying, nourishing. "O taste and see that the Lord is good," (Psalm 34:8). How great a sin, then, for the people in the wilderness to *loathe* the manna! What a disgrace for the church to turn its nose up at God's provision! They murmured against it, and God's wrath fell upon them. Fire consumed the edges of the camp. Plagues swept through them. The very flesh they lusted after, the quails they longed for instead of God's bread, became their judgment—while the meat was still in their mouths, his wrath struck them down (Num. 11:1, 33). They scorned the bread from heaven, and they perished.

And is it any different today? The church in the wilderness of this world is no better. Many who profess Christ still prefer the wares of the world over the Bread of Life. They murmur, they long for things God has not provided, they take *lightly* the grace set before them. But the true church, the remnant of faith, cries out, "Lord, evermore give us this bread," (John 6:34). They see Christ for who he is. They do not loathe him; they hunger for him. They gather him up as their daily bread, knowing that in him is life eternal.

Christ is given to his church, those bought with his own blood, the Savior of his own body (Eph. 5:23). He came to save his people from their sins (Matt. 1:21), and oh, how they need saving! How they need help! In this life, the truth must be continually preached, because even among the professing, there is murmuring. There is discontent. But in heaven, no more explanations will be necessary. No more pleadings, no more rebukes. There, the saints will feast on Christ forever with full understanding, without the temptations of the flesh to distract them.

Yet here, in the wilderness, they must take the Bread from heaven. They must gather it daily, receive it through the means God has ordained. It is given freely, but it must be taken. They must partake of Christ in his word, in prayer, in the sacraments, in the preaching of the gospel. God has provided for his people the suffering Savior, the one sent from heaven to endure divine wrath in the place of sinners. He is the propitiation, the satisfaction, the great covenantal wonder by which sin is removed and God's justice is upheld. But woe to those who refuse him. Woe to those who will *not eat* the manna of God. They are rebels, criminals against the Most High. To them, Christ is not the savor of life, but the savor of death. He becomes to them "a stone of stumbling, and a rock of offence," (1 Peter 2:8). If they will not have him as their bread, they will have him as their judge. If they will not take him as their Savior, they will meet him as their executioner. And what is left for them but fiery serpents? What is left for them but the fate of those in the wilderness who loathed God's provision? Their end is death.

And yet, for those who believe, there is life. "To him that overcometh will I give to eat of the hidden manna," (Rev. 2:17). Christ is the hidden manna, reserved for his people, stored safely in the golden pot of God's covenant. He is given as food, and he is given as a treasure. He is both sustenance and glory. The golden pot testifies to this—it presses the believer to consider that all precious things pertaining to Christ's covenant are kept safe for those who will, by faith, take hold of them.

Inside the ark, beneath the mercy seat, under the glory cloud, before the face of the Most High, there is the manna. It is there for a testimony. It is there as a sacred provision. And what does it say? It says that God has fed his people. He has kept his promises. He has given them life in the wilderness, and he will bring them safely home.

This is the golden pot that holds the manna. This is the ark that secures the *provision* of God. And here, in the presence of divine holiness, is all the abundance of Christ—his fullness, his sufficiency, his eternal supply of grace. "Come unto me, all ye that labour and are heavy laden, and I will give you rest," (Matt. 11:28). It is an invitation, a promise, and a guarantee.

And so, what is the manna? It is *Christ*. What is the golden pot? It is *Christ*. What is the ark of the covenant? It is *Christ*. And what are those who take hold of him? They are the blessed ones, the ones who will never hunger again.

Christ *ought* to be the desire of the ages, the one longed for by all who hunger and thirst for righteousness. "For the bread of God is he which cometh down from heaven, and giveth life unto the world. Then said they unto him, Lord, evermore give us this bread," (John 6:33-34). They desired it, though they did not fully understand what they asked for. But the desire itself, even if imperfect, speaks to the deep and desperate need of mankind. From the beginning, the world has been a wilderness, barren and lifeless without God. And yet, in the midst of it, a provision has been made—manna has rained down, the Bread of Life has come.

The most holy place, the *Sanctum Sanctorum* of the earthly tabernacle, was but a shadow of a greater reality, a representation of the heavenly sanctuary where Christ, the High Priest of an everlasting order, has entered once for all who believe. The writer of Hebrews explains this in careful detail. Beyond the second veil lay the Holiest of all, where the ark of the covenant rested, containing the golden pot of manna, the testimony of God's provision. Year after year, the priest would enter the first tabernacle, performing the service of God. But only once a year, and only the high priest alone, could the second veil be passed. And even then, it was not without blood.

In all of this, the Spirit testified that the way into the *true* Holiest of all was not yet made manifest. The sanctuary remained hidden, the way barred. The manna remained out of sight, stored away, unseen by the people. The provision was there, but it was not yet fully revealed. But now—now the Bread has come down from heaven. Now, the sanctuary is not closed, but opened. The veil is torn, and access is granted. The High Priest has entered, not for himself, but for his people. He has brought the atoning blood, and now, the holiest of places is no longer off-limits.

But as the manna in the wilderness was given for a limited time, to be gathered for a limited time, to be eaten for a limited time, so too is the Bread of Life to be sought while it may still be found. "Seek ye the Lord while he may be found, call ye upon him while he is near," (Isaiah 55:6). Paul echoes the urgency: "This is the accepted time; behold, now is the day of salvation," (2 Cor. 6:2). The gathering must take place. The eating must be done. There is a time to seek, and there is a time when the window of opportunity will close.

The golden pot of manna was a divine act of preservation, a testimony of God's faithfulness. Bread from heaven, given by God's own hand, was kept from corruption by his divine decree. It was sealed away in the ark, a treasure in the most holy place, preserved for all generations as a witness to his provision. So it is with Christ. He is given, ordained by the Father, set apart for the service of God. He does not perish, he does not fade, he does not fail. But he is given for a time, revealed for a time, and must be gathered while the offer stands. Those who take him will be fed. Those who let him lie will find nothing but emptiness when they hunger. The Bread of Life is here—take and eat, lest the opportunity be lost forever. "This is the bread which cometh down from heaven, that a man may eat thereof, and not die," (John 6:50). Christ is the *true* Manna, the Bread of Life, given for you. He is prepared, made fit for your soul, the provision of God's covenant, perfectly suited to the salvation of sinners like us. This Bread is not something you can produce in yourself. It is not something you can earn. It is a gift, given freely, and if you do not take it as God has given it, you will starve with the bread of life so near to you.

Christ is pleasant to those who know their need. He renews your strength. He preserves your life. Just as all men need physical bread, so all men need Christ. The rich and the poor, kings and beggars alike—no one is above their need for the Bread of Life. The Lord Jesus was prepared by the Father for you. He is God's Beloved Son, the one in whom the Father is well pleased—but are you well pleased in him? Do you hunger for him as the Bread of Heaven? Do you see in him all that is needful for your soul? Or do you look for something else, something easier, something more suited to your own liking?

If you do not gather this Manna for yourself, if you do not take hold of Christ, then all his excellence, all his suitability, all his goodness will be of no use to you. A feast spread before you does no good *if you do not eat*. The Prodigal Son would have starved had he not returned to his father's house for bread. The Gospel is a royal banquet, but only those who come to the table will taste its goodness. Christ is sweet to the hungry, precious as gold refined in the fire, as Manna stored in a golden pot for your nourishment. "Unto you therefore which believe he is precious," (1 Peter 2:7).

Just as the Israelites gathered the Manna each day and lived, so you must gather Christ, seeking him, laying hold of him, pressing into him. His work and merit are applied to you by the Spirit, and without him, you can do nothing (John 15:5). Without him, you will die. But with him, your soul is renewed, strengthened, and preserved.

Christ is given freely to all who will take him. The Father has provided this Bread from heaven for your soul. Do you understand what a blessing this is? "Whom have I in heaven but thee? and there is none upon earth that I desire beside thee," (Psalm 73:25). Christ is not just a doctrine to be studied or a name to be admired from a distance. He is Manna—food for your soul, a provision for your hunger, the answer to your need. Unless you taste and see that the Lord is good, unless you eat the flesh of the Son of Man and drink his blood—unless you enter into real, living communion with Christ—all your knowledge of him will be useless. Hearing of Christ, reading of Christ, thinking about Christ will do you no good unless you take him for yourself.

There is no joy apart from this Manna. You may seek happiness elsewhere, but you will not find it. The world is a wilderness, a barren place where nothing can nourish your soul. If you try to live without Christ, you will find only worry, anxiety, discontentment, and dissatisfaction. But if you take this Bread, if you press into the kingdom, if you take Christ by faith, then you will have life. He is the Manna in the golden pot, durable, unchanging, always sufficient. He *is* the same yesterday, today, and forever.

This Manna teaches us something about God's great goodness. The Father has provided the best of all gifts in his Son. And yet, how many refuse him? How many profess to be Christians and yet loathe Christ in their hearts? They do not want him *as he is given*. They want a Christ of their *own* making, a Christ who does not demand too much, who does not rule as King. But the Bread of Life does not come on your terms—it comes on God's. You must take Christ as he is given, or you will have no part in him.

This Manna also teaches us the necessity of coming to Christ. He is food for your soul, and without him, you will perish. To reject him is to choose the fiery serpents, the judgment of God, the condemnation of the wilderness. But to receive him is to enter into life, to eat of the hidden Manna, to be nourished and strengthened until at last, you enter the land of promise, the heavenly Canaan.

Christ is your provision. He is the Manna from heaven, the Bread that gives life. "Whosoever hath the Son, hath the Father also," and whoever eats of this Bread shall never die (John 6:50). He calls to you, "To him that overcometh, will I give to eat of the hidden Manna," (Revelation 2:17). What more do you need? What more could God do for you? Here is food for your soul, freely given, perfectly suited, always sufficient.

Like the Manna in the wilderness, Christ is a mystery to the world. He is food prepared by God, come down from heaven, pure, round, perfect, a gift given freely to all who will take it. He is pleasant to the soul, nourishing, plentiful, equal for all who belong to him, given to his people and no others, sustaining them in their journey through this world until they reach heaven at last. And yet, even with such a gift, those who refuse to eat will starve.

Is not Jesus Christ the wonder of wonders, the Manna given for you? He is prepared by God, a perfect and infinite gift, sent to Jew and Gentile alike, to the small and great, the rich and the poor. He is pleasant, sweet, satisfying. He is sufficient, having enough in him to sustain all his people. And he is given equally to all, justifying his people fully before the Father. There is no other food for your soul. There is no other sustenance in this world but to live on Christ by faith.

And if you would have the saving benefits of this Manna, you *must* eat. You must take him for yourself. You must receive him by faith. For those who eat of this Bread, there is life. For those who refuse, there is only death.

Christ is the Manna for your soul. He is not given to those who reject him but to those who are truly his. And he is always found by those who seek him rightly. If you eat of this Bread, you shall never die, for you have passed from death to life.

If all of this is true—and it is—then it should move you. It should press you toward *holiness*, toward obedience, toward a greater hunger for Christ. The Law is for your good, because the Law is the Word, and the Word is Christ. The Manna is for your good, because Jesus Christ is the hidden Manna, the lively Bread, given for the good of his covenant people. Take him. Gather him. Eat of him. *And live.*

Chapter 4: The Rod

"And after the second veil, the tabernacle which is called the Holiest of all; Which had the golden censer, and the ark of the covenant overlaid round about with gold, wherein was the golden pot that had manna, and Aaron's rod that budded, and the tables of the covenant; and over it the cherubims of glory shadowing the mercyseat; of which we cannot now speak particularly," (Heb. 9:3-5).

The Holiest of all, the most sacred place behind the second veil, held the Ark of the Covenant, covered entirely in gold, a testimony of God's holiness and majesty. Inside this ark lay three significant items: the tablets of the Law, Aaron's rod that budded, and the golden pot of manna. These were not merely relics of Israel's history but tangible signs of God's covenant dealings with his people, each carrying deep significance.

Jonathan Edwards noted that the Apostle Paul, in Hebrews 9:3–5, does not elaborate on the meaning of these objects but instead states, "of which we cannot now speak particularly."[5] Edwards explains that this indicates their *typological* nature, representing evangelical and heavenly things. Some truths remain partially veiled, requiring deep contemplation, much like Peter acknowledged that Paul's

---

[5] Jonathan Edwards, "'Types of the Messiah,'" in *Typological Writings*, ed. Mason I. Lowance Jr. and David H. Watters, vol. 11, The Works of Jonathan Edwards (New Haven; London: Yale University Press, 1993), 323.

writings contained things "hard to be understood" (2 Peter 3:16). The budded rod of Aaron, set in the ark, is one such mystery worth considering.

Inside the Ark was Aaron's rod. Aaron, the son of Amram, was uniquely chosen by God to be the high priest, his name possibly meaning "light bringer" or "mountain of praise." He was not self-appointed; his priesthood was not a position he took by ambition but one to which he was divinely called, as affirmed in Hebrews 5:4. His role was essential, especially in tending the Ark of the Covenant: "And when the camp setteth forward, Aaron shall come, and his sons, and they shall take down the covering vail, and cover the ark of testimony with it," (Numbers 4:5).

Aaron and Moses were given distinct gifts. Moses carried the spirit of governance, while Aaron had the gift of speech. They needed each other. Moses, slow of speech, relied on Aaron's eloquence, while Aaron, lacking the authority of direct leadership, depended on Moses' divine commission. God set this order in place: "And he shall be thy spokesman unto the people: and he shall be, even he shall be to thee instead of a mouth, and thou shalt be to him instead of God," (Exodus 4:16). This order, however, would be challenged.

The inclusion of Aaron's rod in the Ark points back to an event recorded in Numbers 16-17. Korah, Dathan, and Abiram, along with 250 prominent men, rose up against Moses and Aaron, questioning their leadership. Their complaint? That Aaron's family alone was set apart as priests. They resented being excluded from the priesthood and sought to overturn the divine order. Their argument mirrored the rebellion found in many hearts: "Why should you have authority? Why should you decide?" It was an issue of jealousy, of pride, of refusing to submit to God's chosen leadership.

God's response was swift *and terrifying*. Moses called for separation from these rebels, and the ground opened up, swallowing them alive (*hell* opened up and took them). Fire from the Lord consumed the 250 men who had joined them. But even after such a display of divine judgment, the people still murmured. They accused Moses and Aaron of causing the deaths of Korah's followers. To settle the matter once and for all, God commanded each tribal leader to bring a rod, with their names inscribed, and lay them before the Ark. The rod of the man whom God had chosen would bud.

When Moses returned the next day, only Aaron's rod had changed—it had not only budded but had also produced blossoms and ripe almonds. This was a *miraculous* confirmation of God's choice. The rod had come from a dead tree; it had been cut off, lifeless. Yet, by divine power, it sprouted and bore fruit, symbolizing God's sovereign election. No human effort or natural process could account for this—it was entirely the work of God.

The almond tree, from which Aaron's rod was likely cut, is known for being the first tree to bloom in spring, heralding new life after the deadness of winter. The Hebrew word for almond means "to awake," fittingly symbolizing resurrection, divine favor, and the vitality of God's chosen servant. Aaron's rod, placed back in the Ark, became a permanent testimony against rebellion. It was a silent witness that God chooses whom he wills, and his choice is not subject to human opinion.

This sign was meant to silence complaints and stop the people from murmuring against God's order. It was not a mere relic but a testimony that the priesthood was a gift of grace, given so that the people could draw near to God without being consumed. In rejecting Aaron, the people had rejected the provision God had made for their approach to him. The rod in the Ark testified that the way to God is not determined by human will but by divine appointment.

The lesson is clear: rebellion against *God's order* is rebellion against *God* himself. The people failed to see that the priesthood was not a privilege for Aaron's benefit but a *provision* for their salvation. Without a mediator, they could not stand before a holy God. The rod was a sign of life out of death, a foreshadowing of Christ, the true High Priest, whose priesthood is established not by human lineage but by divine decree. And like Aaron's rod, Christ, though crucified and buried, was raised to life, bearing fruit in his resurrection.

Thus, the rod in the Ark is a testimony to us. It is a warning against rejecting *God's appointed means* of salvation. It is a reminder that only through God's chosen High Priest can we approach him. And it is a picture of resurrection life—the evidence that God brings life out of death and establishes his kingdom not by human effort but by his sovereign will. The question is, will we murmur against his order, or will we submit to his perfect plan?

Chapter 4: The Rod

Doctrine: God takes that which is dead and makes it alive for his own glory.

The rod that God directed the people to take was not a long staff but a scepter-like symbol of authority. In Scripture, rods are often associated with rule, discipline, and divine authority. A rod was carried before rulers as a sign of their dignity and governance, and it often represented correction and chastisement. Paul used this imagery in 1 Corinthians 4:21 when he asked, "Shall I come to you with a rod?" The rod could be a symbol of anger, as seen in Isaiah 10:5, where God calls the Assyrian king "the rod of mine anger." It could also signify the power of God's righteous rule, as in Revelation 2:27: "And he shall rule them with a rod of iron." This was not a weak or symbolic rule—it was an unbreakable authority that would subdue all opposition.

The rod could also signify guidance, such as in Psalm 23:4: "Thy rod and thy staff, they comfort me." The staff, with its hook, was for leading; the rod, often a weapon, was for correction. The rod could be a tool of discipline, as seen in Proverbs 13:24: "He that spareth his rod hateth his son." It was also used as a picture of God's authority in preaching, for Isaiah 11:4 says that Christ, "shall smite the earth with the rod of his mouth." The rod represented God's government, his chastisement, his correction, and his Word.

When God commanded that each tribe bring a rod and place their names on it, he was setting up a test of divine appointment. The rods were nothing more than dry sticks—lifeless wood, cut off from their source. They were placed before the Ark of the Covenant, and by the next day, Aaron's rod had budded, bringing forth almonds. This miraculous event demonstrated God's choice of Aaron as the high priest. His rod, though dead, was made alive, bearing fruit.

This rod, like the Ark and the manna, pointed to *Christ*. He, too, was a withered branch, coming in lowliness, despised and rejected. Zechariah prophesied of him, calling him "the Branch" (Zechariah 3:8, 6:12), and Isaiah 11:1 declares, "There shall come forth a rod out of the stem of Jesse." Jesus came in the form of a servant, appearing ordinary, much like any other man. He was cut off, like a lifeless branch, and laid in a tomb. But then, by the power of God, he rose again—he budded, he blossomed, he bore fruit. Aaron's rod was a sign to the rebels, a testimony that God had chosen him and not another. In the same way, Christ's resurrection is the ultimate sign that he alone is the appointed Savior, the High Priest, and the Mediator between God and man. He was vindicated by his works, by his preaching, by his resurrection, and by his ascension. His priesthood is not one of man's appointment but of God's eternal decree.

Just as Aaron's rod was placed in the Ark as a testimony, Christ stands before the throne of God as the everlasting witness to God's covenant. He is near the bread of heaven, near the law, near the mercy seat of atonement. His resurrection, like the budding rod, proves that life has come from death, and that he is the true and eternal High Priest. The question remains: Will you recognize his authority, or will you murmur against God's appointed

Savior as those in the wilderness did? Will you submit to his rule, or will you be among those who resist the rod of his governance? The answer determines whether you stand under his grace or under his judgment.

The rod may also, in some measure, be applied to the mystical body of Christ's covenanted church, which, by its nature in covenant, is first "dead in sin" (Ephesians 2:1); dead sticks. God takes that which is dead and makes it alive. By original sin, Adam and Eve fell from their original righteousness and communion with God and became dead in sin, wholly defiled in all the faculties and parts of soul and body.[6] This corruption affects the whole soul. It consists in the loss of original righteousness and the consequent moral depravity of man's nature. Men are always inclined toward evil, and this is why Scripture describes them as "dead in sin" rather than merely sick. A dead thing has *no* life in itself.

That sin is properly described as death is evident throughout Scripture. It is like a dry, dead stick—void of life, incapable of bearing fruit. Sin so pervades human nature that it renders the soul spiritually dead, making the natural, unrenewed man entirely unable to do anything good in the sight of God. He will always be as Korah, rebelling against God's order. Aaron brought a dead stick—why? Because he had no power to bring one that was alive. He was as bound as the rest of the families to bring that which was dead. Demonstrating the reality of this truth scripturally is simple, as it appears on almost every page of the Bible.

---

[6] *1647 Westminster Confession of Faith*, 6.

1 Kings 8:46 says, "There is no man that sinneth not." Ecclesiastes 7:20 states, "There is not a just man upon earth, that doeth good, and sinneth not." Isaiah 53:6 declares, "All we like sheep have gone astray; we have turned every one to his own way." Even those who think they do righteous deeds, Isaiah 64:6 says, "We are all as an unclean thing, and all our righteousnesses are as filthy rags." Paul, in Romans 3:19, makes a universal statement: "The whole world is guilty before God," and in verses 22-23, "There is no difference: for all have sinned and come short of the glory of God." He affirms this in Galatians 3:22: "The Scripture hath concluded all under sin." All men are under the power and condemnation of sin. The Bible everywhere addresses men as sinners, as *Korahs*; and the ground is always ready to swallow them up. The religion of the Bible is only for sinners. Jesus Christ came to save his people *from* their sins. If men are not sinners, there is no need for Christ as the Savior of men. The bad news must come first, then the good news that God is sovereign and he can reverse the fall through Christ.

The entire human race, by its apostasy from God in Adam, is completely depraved in every faculty and part of its being. People despise this doctrine, yet it is foundational to knowing both themselves and God. Without it, one cannot understand the Redeemer. Original sin teaches that men are entirely deprived of holiness and cannot perform righteousness in any way. No unrenewed man understands or seeks after God. The thoughts of his heart are only evil continually. In this way, men live without God—they are practical atheists. This alienation is so great and universal that Scripture says men are the enemies of God (Romans 5:10). Ephesians 2:3 states, "We also were by nature the children of wrath, even as others," picturing men as spiritually dead in sin. Paul writes, "The natural man receiveth not the things of the Spirit of God: for they are foolishness unto him: neither can he know them; because they are spiritually discerned," (1 Corinthians 2:14). Again, in Ephesians 2:1 and 5, he says, "You hath he quickened who were dead in trespasses and sins...even us..." who need to be "quickened together with Christ." Dead sticks lying before the ark of the testimony—only one came alive. Only *one* was found in the ark.

All men are dead in sin, dry sticks, spiritually lifeless. What does spiritual death mean? 1 Corinthians 15:22 states, "In Adam all die." This refers to being in and under the covenant Adam broke. Ephesians 2:1–3 clarifies, "And you were dead in the trespasses and sins in which you once walked, ... and were by nature children of wrath, like the rest of mankind." Why does the world desire evil? Natural human dispositions from conception are bound to Adam. People are born in the likeness of Adam and are naturally disobedient. They are, by nature, children upon whom God will pour out his wrath—children of wrath. Paul further explains in Ephesians 4:18, "Having the understanding darkened, being alienated from the life of God through the ignorance that is in them, because of the blindness of their heart," (Ephesians 4:18). They are separated and alienated from God. They are insensible to spiritual good. They are wholly incapable of any act of true life or righteousness. The 1647 Westminster Confession of Faith states that people are, "made opposite to all good, and wholly inclined to all evil" (6:4). That means they cannot do good; they only do evil—until God causes them to bud and come alive.

God rescues people by supernatural providence, just as he did with Aaron's rod. When it is said that God rescues sinners, it means he causes them to pass from death to life. He takes that which is dead and makes it alive—before they do anything. Notice that first the rod must bud, then sprout, then grow, then bear fruit, and finally, be placed in the ark. Alive first, then growing. This change is accomplished by God in a moment. There is no intermediate state between lost and saved. There is no *lengthy transition* between being a dead stick and a living branch. When God changes a person, they are *changed*, and lasting fruit will come from it.

Scripture divides all of mankind into two classes: wise and foolish; sheep and goats; saved and lost. Matthew 25:2 likens people to wise and foolish virgins: "Five of them were foolish, and five were wise." Jesus again divides people into two groups—sheep and goats—when he says, "And he will place the sheep on his right, but the goats on the left," (Matthew 25:33). There is no preparation, no in-between state. There are simply two classes: sticks that are alive and sticks that remain dead. When God changes a person's heart, he gives them spiritual life—something they did not have before.

Paul affirms this in Ephesians 4:8-9: "Wherefore he saith, When he ascended up on high, he led captivity captive, and gave gifts unto men." Here, he quotes Psalm 68:18: "Thou hast ascended on high, thou hast led captivity captive: thou hast received gifts for men; yea, for the rebellious also, that the LORD God might dwell among them." The Psalmist is speaking of God's works. Paul interprets this as Christ's work in his ascension. In Christ's redemption, he gives gifts to men and leads captivity (those dead in sin) captive (now free in Christ). The work of God is attributed to Christ, and always according to his life-giving covenant, for he alone is High Priest.

How does God make alive that which is dead? The budding of Aaron's rod, blossoming and bearing fruit, is a type of God's ordained prescriptions and his blessing upon his ministry. Aaron's rod was of an almond tree (Numbers 17:8), which God uses in Jeremiah 1:11–12 as a token and type of his Word, which takes effect speedily, just as Aaron's rod quickly bore fruit.

Two things must be noted. First, God only blesses his ordained means. All the rods did not bloom—only Aaron's, the one chosen by God. Second, Aaron's rod was placed in the ark to show God's favor upon his ministry. This truth stretches across all doctrines, all aspects of church life, family life, devotion, salvation, and ministry. God does not desire mere budding or blossoming, but fruit-bearing. Does this not enhance what Christ says about branches bearing fruit? "I am the vine, ye are the branches: He that abideth in me, and I in him, the same bringeth forth much fruit: for without me ye can do nothing," (John 15:5). Christians are twigs grafted into the vine—what began as a rod becomes fruitful by God's ordination.

What does Christ say next about branches that do not bear fruit? "If a man abide not in me, he is cast forth as a branch, and is withered; and men gather them, and cast them into the fire, and they are burned," (John 15:6). What happened to Korah happens to them. God can make that which is dry flourish with life, as he did with Aaron's rod, as he did with Sarah's barren womb. If God but speaks the word, it is done, for there is mighty efficacy in God's Word and his prescribed ordinances. He makes the *dead* come alive.

The rule of souls begins with the reality that those who truly encounter God have the life of God in their souls. He rules your soul by his rod—by his Son and by his word. The fall of man set the stage for this need, for though Adam was given life in the garden, he lost it through disobedience. Life was removed, and we all became dead sticks. A new principle of life had to be implanted. Dead sticks must be resurrected, and if they are truly brought to life, they will bear fruit—because fruitfulness *proves* life.

The Christian's encounter with the living God is not just an idea or a theory; it is a supernatural work of the Spirit applying the work of Christ. Abraham is used in Romans and Galatians as the father of our faith, and Genesis gives us the foundational example of what it means to be brought to life by God. The living God interacts with his creation to make them holy and fruitful, but first, he must instill life in what is dead. Pharaoh was not a follower of God—Abraham was. Laban was not a follower of God—Jacob was. The line between the seed of the woman and the seed of the serpent is drawn in permanent ink. One has life, the other remains dead. One is a dry stick, the other blossoms by the rod of Jesse.

The New Testament echoes this truth—this implanted life—again and again. The living God does not merely reform people; he intrudes into their deadness and makes them alive. Jesus says in John 10:28, "And I give them eternal life, and they shall never perish; neither shall any man pluck them out of my hand." The eternal, living God implants eternal life in us. It is not borrowed or temporary; it is as permanent as the life of God himself. That's why Christ calls it living water, flowing from those who have been born again. Peter understood this when he said, "And we believe and are sure that thou art that Christ, the Son of the living God," (John 6:69). Jesus Christ is the Son of the living God.

God's plan is not simply to inspire people or call them to morality—he comes to personally intervene, to make dead things live. He does this in such a remarkable way that he not only dies and is buried but proves his power by rising from the dead. Resurrection equals life. A dead stick brought to life. The living God raised Christ from the dead because salvation and victory over death are accomplished by the very principle of God's necessary being—life itself. But not everyone has this life. When the rods were laid before the ark, only one came alive. As Christ says, not everyone has this life (John 6:53). It must be given, implanted by the living God. Otherwise, men remain dead in sin—just as those other sticks remained lifeless. But when God gives life, dead sticks will blossom. As Paul says in Romans 9:26, "And it shall come to pass, that in the place where it was said unto them, Ye are not my people; there shall they be called the children of the living God."

When God gives life, we experience his indwelling power and enter into a covenant relationship with him through Jesus Christ. Paul declares, "For ye are the temple of the living God," (2 Corinthians 6:16). As God has said, "I will dwell in them, and walk in them; and I will be their God, and they shall be my people," (2 Corinthians 6:16). If you have encountered the living God, if his life has been implanted in you, then your life will reflect that reality. It will not be something you merely affirm; it will be something you live. Those who are made alive by God cannot continue in their old ways. Paul writes that those who are still in sin—adulterers, fornicators, idolaters, manipulators, haters, jealous, angry, selfish, envious, murderers, drunkards—will not inherit the kingdom of God (Galatians 5:19-21). There is no use for dead sticks in the holy of holies.

Religion is drudgery for the wicked because they have no life. That's why they see it as a crutch, something for weak people. But if you have encountered the living God, how could prayer be boring? How could the gathering of the saints in worship be dull? Unless, of course, you are still dead. The Bible doesn't just tell us about the living God—it shows us, through history, the importance of walking in covenant life rather than in self-reliance. What do you trust? Laban ran to his household idols. Pharaoh turned to his magicians. Abraham, before he was converted, was a worshiper of pagan gods. And men today still worship idols—they just look different. Their jobs, their friends, their money, their possessions, their own opinions—all are gods they cling to, just as the pagans did. But true satisfaction is only found in the living God, the one who brings dead things to life.

It is a tragedy that some professing Christians believe they played a part in their conversion. They fail to grasp the immense wonder of what God has done. Can you imagine all the things they will never understand in Scripture because they refuse to believe they were truly dead? They miss everything.

God speaks, and things live. His word is not just information—it is life. Deuteronomy 8:3 declares, "Man doth not live by bread only, but by every word that proceedeth out of the mouth of the LORD doth man live." Christ himself used these words to defeat the devil in the wilderness. Men live by the word of the living God, and Christ is that living word. He is the *Life-giver*.

Is it a comfort to you to know that the same God who made Aaron's rod blossom is at work in you? Do you see that he deals with you as he did with his people of old? Has he taken a dead stick and made it alive for you? Do you know that his resurrection power is as true for you as it was for those he has made alive throughout history? Christ, the

Branch of Righteousness, has engrafted you into himself. The rod is a picture of two things—Christ as the rod of God, and us as dead sticks made alive.

He hides you inside his ark, under the wings of his love and mercy, covered by the covenant. But if you are stubborn, if you resist his rule, he will govern you with the rod. He disciplines his people, not to destroy them, but to refine them. The Lord teaches his saints through trials, causing them to grow, to bear fruit. Those who refuse to bear fruit are cut off. "Every branch in me that beareth not fruit he taketh away," (John 15:2). Jesus cursed the barren fig tree, and it immediately withered. It claimed to have fruit but had none. He will bring life to a dead stick, but he will not tolerate deception—an appearance of life without true fruit.

Some are cut off suddenly, struck down by God's judgment. Others fade spiritually, becoming lean in their souls. Some are excommunicated, removed from the visible church. But all of it is a picture of what ought to happen, and where it ought to happen—in holiness, before the ark, where the bread is, where the law is, where the mercy seat is. It is there that God makes dead sticks live.

So go on. *Persevere.* Press forward in God's work among you. Not just to see the buds, or even the blossoms, but to see the fruit. Aaron's rod had buds, blossoms, and fruit all at once. How? By sound doctrine, by the Spirit's power, by the life-giving grace of God. That is what it means to grow, to be built up in holiness, to walk in truth, to be

Chapter 4: The Rod

knit together in one body under Christ, bound together in love.

It is not by accident that God did not leave the rod outside the ark but placed it inside—next to the bread, near the law, under the mercy seat, in his presence. That is where he places you, hidden in Christ. Paul explains it: "Thou, being a wild olive tree, wert graffed in among them, and with them partakest of the root and fatness of the olive tree," (Romans 11:17). You are grafted into the covenant. God alone takes dead things and brings them to life.

And yet, for all the comfort and help we receive from these truths, the rod of God also signifies rebuke and judgment. "Let him take his rod away from me," (Job 9:34), Job said. The Assyrian king was called the rod of God's anger (Isaiah 10:5). God's word against the wicked is described in Psalm 2:9: "Thou shalt break them with a rod of iron." Those who refuse his grace will meet his wrath. Those who will not submit to his rule will be broken by his judgment.

A branch severed from the tree cannot live. Christ said, "Without me ye can do nothing," (John 15:5). But by grace, by the miracle of the gospel, God takes dead sticks and makes them live. May we all be branches full of life, bearing fruit for his glory.

Chapter 5: The Mercy Seat

"And after the second veil, the tabernacle which is called the Holiest of all; Which had the golden censer, and the ark of the covenant overlaid round about with gold, wherein was the golden pot that had manna, and Aaron's rod that budded, and the tables of the covenant; and over it the cherubims of glory shadowing the mercyseat; of which we cannot now speak particularly," (Heb. 9:3-5).

The passage in Hebrews 9:3-5 gives us a glimpse into the most sacred place in Israel's worship—the Holy of Holies. "And after the second veil, the tabernacle which is called the Holiest of all; Which had the golden censer, and the ark of the covenant overlaid round about with gold, wherein was the golden pot that had manna, and Aaron's rod that budded, and the tables of the covenant; and over it the cherubims of glory shadowing the mercy seat; of which we cannot now speak particularly," (Hebrews 9:3-5).

Beyond the second veil, behind the heavy curtain, was the chamber of absolute holiness—the Holy of Holies. Within it stood the ark of the covenant, a box of acacia wood overlaid with pure gold, both inside and out. The ark was more than an object; it was a throne, a meeting place between the Most High and his people. Three sacred items were housed within it—the tablets of the Law, Aaron's rod that budded, and the golden pot of manna. These were not mere relics of the past; they were testimonies of God's covenant dealings with Israel, and they sat beneath the mercy seat—the place where God's presence hovered in shekinah glory.

Atop the ark was its crown, the mercy seat. The Greek word used in Hebrews 9:5 is ἱλαστήριον (hilasterion), which means a place of appeasement, an expiatory covering, a propitiation. The writer of Hebrews connects this to the cover of the ark, the place where the blood of atonement was sprinkled on the Day of Atonement. The significance was staggering—here was the place where Israel's sins were symbolically removed, where their deserved judgment was transferred to the sacrifice, where God was satisfied.

Exodus 25 describes the construction and purpose of this mercy seat: "And thou shalt make a mercy seat of pure gold: two cubits and a half shall be the length thereof, and a cubit and a half the breadth thereof. And thou shalt make two cherubims of gold, of beaten work shalt thou make them, in the two ends of the mercy seat. And make one cherub on the one end, and the other cherub on the other end: even of the mercy seat shall ye make the cherubims on the two ends thereof. And the cherubims shall stretch forth their wings on high, covering the mercy seat with their wings, and their faces shall look one to another; toward the mercy seat shall the faces of the cherubims be. And thou shalt put the mercy seat above upon the ark; and in the ark thou shalt put the testimony that I shall give thee. And there I will meet with thee, and I will commune with thee from above the mercy seat, from between the two cherubims which are upon the ark of the testimony, of all things which

I will give thee in commandment unto the children of Israel," (Exodus 25:17-22).

The very name *mercy seat* speaks volumes. The Hebrew word for it comes from a verb meaning "to cover." It was a place of expiation, where sin was covered, atoned for, and removed. The blood sprinkled there was not just a ritual; it was a declaration that sin demands death, but God provides mercy through a substitute.

This golden lid was precisely measured to fit the ark, a reminder that God's atonement is exact, not haphazard. It covered the testimony—the Law—which stood as a witness against sinners. Without it, the Law would only condemn; with it, there was a mediator between God and man. "For all have sinned, and come short of the glory of God," (Romans 3:23), but some will find mercy at the mercy seat.

And what was the purpose of this mercy seat? God himself tells us: "There I will meet with thee, and I will commune with thee, from above the mercy-seat," (Exodus 25:22). This was where God met with his people—not at the Law, not at the judgment seat, but at the mercy seat. It was there that he spoke, where he ruled, where he atoned, and where grace was found. Numbers 7:89 records, "And when Moses was gone into the tabernacle of the congregation to speak with him, then he heard the voice of one speaking unto him from off the mercy seat that was upon the ark of testimony, from between the two cherubims: and he spake unto him."

The mercy seat was the *throne* of the Lord of Hosts, who is called, "the Lord which dwelleth between the cherubims," (1 Samuel 4:4; Psalm 80:1; Isaiah 37:16). The presence of God was not found in the abstract—it was centered at the mercy seat, where his justice and his mercy met.

The doctrine drawn from this passage is clear: *Christians find forgiveness of sins and acceptance before God at the throne of grace.* But how does one move from the idea of the propitiatory sacrifice, found in mercy, to this throne of grace?

By way of allusion, the mercy seat itself is a throne. It is the very chariot throne of Christ, a throne not merely of justice but of mercy. It is a golden crown where he sits, attended by cherubim, ruling from the place of atonement. Beneath him lies the testimony of the Law—his righteous standard, his covenant with his people—and the provisions of life in the golden pot of manna and Aaron's rod that budded. The ark of the covenant was mobile, moving and settling among his people, demonstrating that his rule and reign were ever-present. Most significantly, it was the place of blood—the most holy place where atonement was made for the sins of his people.

And yet, this mercy seat is not an annual visitation, as in the days of Israel's high priest, but a continual invitation. The Christian is called to come—not once a year, not only in crisis, but moment by moment—to find grace to help in time of need. This is precisely why the writer of Hebrews first speaks of the throne of grace before expounding how such a throne is established in Christ. As William Gouge put it: "Christ himself, his body was the truth of the Tabernacle: his deity, of the Altar; his human nature, of the sacrifice: his person of the Priest: his graces were the truth of the priests' robes: his mediation the truth of the incense: he is the true mercy seat, he the Ark; he the Manna: he the water that flowed out of the rock: he the truth of types. Heaven was the truth of the most holy place."[7]

The Throne of Grace

First, we must recognize that there is indeed a throne of grace. It is typified by the mercy seat, the place where the Lord met with his people. "(For the LORD thy God is a merciful God;) he will not forsake thee, neither destroy thee, nor forget the covenant of thy fathers which he sware unto them," (Deuteronomy 4:31). This passage, set in the context of God's covenant dealings with his people, teaches that even when they fall into sin and are driven from the land, if they return to the Lord, they will find mercy (Deuteronomy 4:25–31).

But this mercy is not arbitrary—it is rooted in God's *covenant faithfulness*. There is a reason God receives the believer. This is not a bare reception, but a specific, gracious act based on the covenant of grace. When sinners seek the Lord, they find mercy, because they are pardoned and forgiven. Why do they need mercy? Because there is a law,

---

[7] William Gouge, *A Learned and Very Useful Commentary on the Whole Epistle to the Hebrews* [London: A.M., T.W. and S.G. for Joshua Kirton, 1655], 390.

and that law must be upheld. A broken covenant demands a remedy, and that remedy is found not in the Covenant of Works, which offers no mercy, but in the Covenant of Grace, where salvation is extended to poor sinners through Christ.

Moses' covenant was gracious, setting forth in types the very throne of mercy we see in Christ. Jesus rebuked the Jews for failing to see this: "Had ye believed Moses, ye would have believed Me; but if ye believe not Moses, how will ye believe My words?" (John 5:46-47). The law, the mercy seat, and the entire system of sacrifices were all pointing to Christ, the fulfillment of the covenant promises.

In this Covenant of Grace, sinners are accepted through unmerited favor, received into mercy through repentance and faith alone: "When thou art in tribulation and all these things are come upon thee in the latter days, if thou turn to the Lord thy God and shalt be obedient to His voice (for the Lord thy God is a merciful God), He will not forsake thee, neither destroy thee, nor forget the covenant of thy fathers which He sware unto them," (Deuteronomy 4:30-31).

This throne is called a throne of *mercy* because God himself is merciful. Pardon of sin is the great privilege of the covenant. As God declared to Moses, "The Lord, the Lord God, merciful, and gracious, long-suffering, and abundant in goodness and truth, keeping mercy for thousands, forgiving iniquity, transgression and sin," (Exodus 34:6-7).

Mercy and Grace Distinguished

Mercy and grace are closely related, yet distinct. *Mercy* is kindness exercised toward the miserable—those in desperate need of rescue. *Grace* is love exercised toward the unworthy. Grace flows from God's love, where he communicates himself freely to sinners without any merit on their part. Mercy is the conduit by which this grace is applied.

Paul emphasizes this when he writes, "He hath mercy on whom he will have mercy," (Romans 9:18). This mercy is not general—it is specific, directed toward those whom God has chosen as "vessels of mercy, which he had afore prepared unto glory," (Romans 9:23). God's mercy is eternal: "With everlasting kindness will I have mercy on thee, saith the LORD thy Redeemer," (Isaiah 54:8). "It is of the LORD'S mercies that we are not consumed, because his compassions fail not," (Lamentations 3:22).

The Role of Christ

At the heart of God's mercy is Christ himself. He is the very cornerstone of the covenant, the means by which sinners may draw near to God. Where will they find him? Seated as King on his throne of mercy. He does not merely rule in justice, though he is just; he rules with grace, dispensing mercy to those in need.

Though God is a consuming fire, "terrible out of his holy places," (Psalm 68:35), Christ is our mediator. He is both the appeaser and the one appeased. That is why men are invited to come boldly to the throne of grace (Hebrews 4:14, 16).

There he sits, adorned with a golden crown of mercy, shining in purity and eternity, captivating his people with his goodness. His throne is perfect, established in righteousness, fitted for his covenant work, and occupied by the One who intercedes for his people. From this throne, he rules, speaks, and ministers grace upon grace. It is a throne where mercy is freely offered, flowing from his heart of compassion. He pities the sinner, not merely as a judge looking upon a criminal, but as a Father gazing upon his helpless child.

At the throne of grace, Jesus does not merely acknowledge sin—he atones for it. He does not merely show kindness—he secures redemption. He does not merely grant access—he welcomes the weary, the broken, and the lost. He sees us in our misery and opens his arms, inviting us to find mercy and grace in our time of need.

And what is this mercy for? It is for sinners, for the unlovely, for the rebels who deserve nothing but judgment. Yet, through Christ, the sentence is lifted, the debt is paid, and grace abounds. Here, at the throne of grace, we find everything we need—atonement, acceptance, and the unshakable promise of eternal life.

As God sits upon his mercy seat, he does so not in cold justice, but in the warmth of divine love, making dead things live, and sustaining all life by the power of his resurrecting hand.

The Lord's throne of grace and his mercy seat are one and the same, a singular place where God's justice and mercy meet. He sits upon a throne, yet it is a throne of mercy, a chariot throne from which he reigns over all. This is no mere relic of Old Testament imagery but the very foundation of New Testament hope. The mercy seat under the Law was the same as the throne of grace under the Gospel. The same God, the same Savior, the same Mediator. The difference? The veil has been torn, and what was once hidden away is now revealed.

The Mercy Seat as the Throne of Christ

The mercy seat was the golden covering of the ark, the place where the blood of the atonement was sprinkled, where God's glory dwelt between the cherubim. And Christ is shown as seated there—dwelling upon the mercy seat as his golden throne. The writer of Hebrews makes it plain: the throne of grace is nothing less than this same mercy seat, the place where God meets with his people.

Understanding the mercy seat is the key to understanding the throne of grace. God, in his majestic glory, set forth strict rules for coming before him. The ark was called his glory (Psalm 78:61), and upon it rested the mercy seat, where he sat enthroned between the cherubim. The angels themselves, those glorious ministers of heaven, were called "cherubims of glory" because they surrounded this throne (Hebrews 9:5). It is the very throne upon which Christ sits, pure and holy, shining forth his righteousness.

When Isaiah beheld Christ upon his throne, the seraphim cried out, "Holy, holy, holy" (Isaiah 6:1). This was none other than the great white throne of God.

From this seat, Christ *reigns* as King. His throne is a chariot throne, a throne of mercy, for no sinner can draw near to God apart from it. Sin has separated man from his Creator. The misery of sin is not merely its guilt, but its consequence: separation from God's holiness. And yet, in Christ, there is a way back—a Mediator has been given, both God and man, Prophet, Priest, and King. He alone stands between God and sinners, offering his blood upon the mercy seat, that they may boldly come before the face of the Father.

From this throne, mercy is extended—but only according to the decree of God. One cannot come to the throne of grace on their own terms. The Father speaks through the Son, and all authority has been given into his hands. "The throne of grace is the throne of God and of the Lamb," (Revelation 22:3). The word "throne" should call to mind the mercy seat, the ark, and all it typified—the propitiation made for sin, the blood sprinkled in atonement, the High Priest who intercedes.

The Blood of Propitiation

To come to the throne of grace is to come before the Father in Christ. It is to employ by faith the work of Christ in mediation, trusting in his blood, his righteousness, his atonement. This is why the blood was sprinkled upon the mercy seat: "He shall sprinkle of the blood upon the mercy seat eastward; and before the mercy seat shall he sprinkle of the blood with his finger seven times," (Leviticus 16:14). Christ is our High Priest, and his sacrifice is the fulfillment of this very act. There is no throne of grace apart from Christ. There is no mercy seat but by his mediation.

King Jesus, our only sovereign and Lord (Jude 4), reigns from this throne. And though it is a throne of mercy to those who come in faith, it is a throne of dread to the wicked. The judgment seat is the mercy seat turned against them. When they finally behold Christ in his glory, seated upon his holy throne, they will see the law they have broken beneath him, and they will have no atonement to cover them, no blood to sprinkle, no Mediator to intercede.

David Clarkson writes, "When he is spoken of as upon his throne, the mercy-seat, he is called the Lord of hosts, one who has all the power in the world, 1 Sam. 4:4, 2 Sam. 6:2. And the ark, whereof the mercy-seat was a principal part, is called the strength of God, Ps. 78:61, and 132:8; because, as it was a testimony of his presence, so a symbol of his strength and power."[8] The very throne of mercy is also the throne of judgment. Those who come to Christ now, in faith, find mercy. Those who reject him will face his judgment, for he will rule the nations with a rod of iron.

The Throne of Holiness

---

[8] David Clarkson, *The Works of David Clarkson*, vol. 3 [Edinburgh: James Nichol, 1864], 113.

God's throne is a throne of mercy, but it is also a throne of holiness. It is called "the throne of his holiness," (Psalm 47:8). The most holy place was the "holiness of holinesses," (Exodus 26:34), and so the mercy seat was the throne of his holiness. Moses came before this throne to inquire of the Lord. It was there that Christ spoke with him. And for Christians today, where do we go for knowledge, for communion, for grace to help in time of need? To the mercy seat. To the throne of grace. This was the sum and substance of the Gospel, held in types and shadows.

And yet, for all the majesty of the mercy seat, it was *hidden* from the people. The high priest alone could enter once a year. The veil separated it, keeping sinners from drawing near. But now, the throne of grace is thrown open. The veil is torn. Access has been granted.

"And the temple of God was opened in heaven, and there was seen in his temple the ark of his testament," (Revelation 11:19). The temple is open, the ark is seen, and Christ sits upon the mercy seat. The veil was torn at the moment of his death (Matthew 27:51), and all who have been atoned for may now come boldly.

To come to the throne of grace is to come to the very presence of God. It is to stand before the throne, not in fear of wrath, but in confidence of mercy. This is because God has been fully satisfied in Christ. His wrath is appeased. His justice is upheld. The law remains, but the blood has been sprinkled. The very name of this throne declares its purpose: grace.

The writer of Hebrews uses the same word for mercy seat when he speaks of Christ: "ἱλαστήριον, a propitiation" (Romans 3:25). Christ is the propitiation for our sins. He is the mercy seat. He is the atonement. He is the way, the truth, and the life.

The blood of the sin-offering was sprinkled upon the mercy seat seven times, a perfect and complete atonement. Christ's blood fully satisfies the justice of God. There is nothing left to add. There is nothing left to do. Through Christ, sinners are reconciled, pardoned, justified.

Come to the Mercy Seat

How foolish it would be to have such a throne of mercy available and yet *not* come! How many souls perish, standing outside the veil, refusing to enter? The mercy seat is not for those who would remain in their sins, who would stand at a distance, who would reject the only atonement God has provided. It is for sinners who will come, who will plead the blood of Christ, who will trust in his sacrifice.

There is no other way. Either we come now, in faith, or we will face the throne in judgment. Christ reigns, and his throne is unshaken. But for those who are his, for those who trust him, for those who come—there is mercy. There is grace. There is acceptance.

Come to the mercy seat. Come to the throne of grace. Christians find grace because his throne is a seat of mercy, covering the tablets of the law with the atonement of Christ. It is here, at the mercy seat, where poor sinners may come boldly, for Christ himself sits and rules by his holiness. The mercy seat is the place where the broken covenant of the law is covered, where Christ, as Mediator, stands between the condemning justice of the Father and the sinner's guilt. "Blessed are they whose iniquities are forgiven, and whose sins are covered," (Romans 4:7). The covering of sin is not an arbitrary act—it is a work of mediation, a work of atonement, where the Father no longer sees the indictments of the law against his people, but instead, sees the blood sprinkled by the red hand of Christ.

From this seat, God looks upon his family, not with condemnation, but through the lens of mercy. The law remains, the justice of God remains, yet the condemning weight of the law is hidden from sight by the work of the Mediator. The mercy seat is the *covering* of the law for those who are in Christ. It is the throne where Christ rules, and where Christians may find help in time of need. It is also the place where communion is established, for what did God tell Moses? "There I will meet with thee, and I will commune with thee from above the mercy seat," (Exodus 25:22). The Lord's Supper itself is a visible sign of this communion, a testimony to the ongoing mercy of Christ toward his people. Christ does not take breaks from his intercession. He is not a priest who entered into the holy place once a year and then left. He is a priest who "ever liveth to make intercession for them," (Hebrews 7:25). The writer of Hebrews builds his entire argument upon this: Christ is greater than all the Old Testament types. He is greater than the angels, greater than Moses, greater than the earthly tabernacle, greater than the blood of bulls and goats, greater than the Aaronic priesthood. And by way of fulfillment, he is the ark, the manna, the law, the mercy seat, and the King who sits upon his throne of grace. The writer even acknowledges that there is so much to say on these things, yet time does not permit it. But here is the great truth: Christ sits there, on his throne of grace, in perpetual communion with sinners who boldly come.

A Throne of Justice and Mercy

It is either one or the other. The throne of Christ is a throne of justice for the covenant breakers or a throne of mercy for those who come by faith. The same throne, the same seat, but two entirely different effects depending on who comes before it. For his people, it is the throne of grace where he abides, "He that sitteth on the throne shall dwell among them," (Revelation 7:15). His presence is not fleeting—it is abiding. He is always ready and willing to show mercy.

Through Christ alone, by his mediation, by his blood, sinners are given access to the Father. The blood of bulls and goats could not truly atone, but only pointed to the true atonement to come. There is an infinite chasm between the sacrifices of the old covenant and the work of Christ, "who came by his own blood." Christ does what the type could not do—he reconciles his people to the Father. His blood proves that there is no access to God apart from the removal of sin and the satisfaction of divine wrath. The blood of God himself was the price for man's covenant-breaking, and through this blood, his people are sanctified. So, what shall we consider as we come to the mercy seat? How should we approach this throne of grace? With high thoughts of the price of our redemption. The blood of Christ was not too dear for the Father to give, nor should it be too little in our own hearts. It is by this blood that Christ entered the true holy place: "By his own blood he entered in once into the holy place, having obtained eternal redemption for us," (Hebrews 9:12). Heaven itself is described as the "holy place," the truth of which the earthly type was but a shadow.

A holy God, seated upon a holy throne, reigning in the most holy place, surrounded by the praises of angels who cry "holy, holy, holy"—this is where Christ sits. This is the seat of mercy, where miserable sinners may come, where grace is found. This is the mercy seat that was foreshadowed in the tabernacle, now revealed in its fullness in the heavenly realm where Christ reigns. Here is where redemption is found. Here is where eternal life is dispensed.

The Mercy Seat as the Fountain of Redemption

Christ did not simply *obtain* redemption—he *distributes* it. His intercession *applies* the benefits of his atoning work. All the blessings of salvation—justification, reconciliation, sanctification—flow from this throne. The picture is clear: the King, seated upon his throne of mercy, dispensing grace to those who boldly come. His ransom was the full price of redemption, freeing his people from all the misery into which sin had plunged them. Through him, sinners are reconciled to the Father, justified by faith, sanctified in their walk, and one day, glorified to be with him in the eternal kingdom, where all things will be made new.

The mercy seat was always a special type of Christ, for he is expressly called our propitiation: "He is the propitiation for our sins," (1 John 2:2). But there is something remarkable about this mercy seat—it is a narrow place. It is not broad. It is not open to any and all who would come by any means they choose. No, the mercy seat is specific. The way to approach God is specific. God does not allow men to come in any way they please, but only through the Mediator he has appointed. The narrow mercy seat signified the way in which God would cover sin—only through Christ.

Through Christ's merits, iniquity is covered. Through Christ's mediation, the Father is merciful. The writer of Hebrews even calls Christ himself the propitiation, the place of atonement, because it is through him that grace is extended to sinners. This favor, this mercy, is found only in him. The mercy seat was placed over the tablets of the law, where God's majesty dwelt between the cherubim, to signify that Christ stands between God's justice and the sinner. The Father looks upon the law, but through Christ—seeing it fulfilled, seeing it satisfied, seeing it covered by atonement.

Boldly Coming to the Throne

This is why we can boldly come. This is why we can stand before God, not in fear, but in confidence—because Christ is there. His blood has been shed. His work is finished. His throne is one of mercy. And in him, we find forgiveness of sins and acceptance before the Father.

To come to the throne of grace is to come to the seat of mercy, to the very throne of the Most High God. There, and only there, is atonement found. There, and only there, is grace given. Let us, then, come boldly to this throne of grace, knowing that in Christ, we are fully accepted.

The Sweetest Thing is to Find Mercy

Mercy is the sweetest thing a soul can experience, but it is not so easily obtained. It does not come apart from justice, for the tablets of the law rest beneath the mercy seat. God's mercy is over his justice, but his wrath against sinners remains as a sword of fire, barring the way back into the garden, guarding against all who break his covenant. When we come boldly to the throne of grace, we do not come apart from Christ. We come through Christ, to Christ, to the Father. We come to a consuming fire, to a throne of holiness, and unless we come clothed in Christ's righteousness, we will be consumed.

How will a man gain mercy? What means shall allow him through this wall of holiness? Only the righteousness and satisfaction of Jesus Christ. If a man comes to Christ's throne without the covering of Christ's righteousness, he will find no safety at that mercy seat. For after death, and at judgment, there will be no more mercy if one is not wrapped in it now. Without being sprinkled with the blood of Christ—offered up to the Father by his eternal Spirit (Hebrews 9:14)—the sinner will find Christ *a terrible Judge*, measuring his soul by the weight of the law, and finding him infinitely lacking.

But for those who come now, those who come boldly to Christ's throne, who seek him at his mercy seat, they will find grace to help in time of need. When the writer of Hebrews tells us to come boldly, it is not a casual invitation. We come to the ark of the covenant. We come to the throne of the mercy seat. We come to the place where Christ dwells in intercession, ruling as King in holiness and grace, giving out mercy to those who are covered by his blood. This is why Hebrews later exhorts: "Let us draw near with a true heart, in full assurance of faith, having our hearts sprinkled from an evil conscience," (Hebrews 10:22).

None come to the holiest place—this throne of holiness—except they are first made ready by that blood of sprinkling which purges their conscience from dead works to serve the living God. If a man is ever to stand before God and see his face in comfort, he must seek Christ now. Robert Rollock spoke to this reality: "Either must he be banished from the presence and face of God for ever, and be cast into the society of the damned, or else if he would be saved, he must be engrafted by a true and lively faith in Jesus Christ."[9]

Yet, how many love mercy but hate holiness? They want the crown, but not the cross. They long for relief from suffering, but they do not desire God's covenant of mercy. They seek deliverance from affliction, but they do not seek Christ who sits upon the seat of mercy.

And what a great sin it is to reject God's mercy! It is greater than the breaking of a commandment, for where there is great mercy, there is great sin when that mercy is despised. The *law* tells us our duty, but gives us *no power* to perform it. But the Covenant of Grace not only commands, it also gives the power to obey. Christ, from his mercy seat, ministers that power through the Spirit. If a man would have mercy, he must come boldly to Christ—but always on God's terms, never his own.

This is why the writer of Hebrews warns only a chapter later: "For if we sin willfully after that we have received the knowledge of the truth, there remaineth no more sacrifice for sins, but a certain fearful looking for of judgment and fiery indignation, which shall devour the adversaries. He that despised Moses' law died without mercy," (Hebrews 10:26-28). Christ's mercy is a rescuing mercy from his mercy seat. It is the only place of safety, the only place where a sinner can find refuge.

Come to the Throne of Grace

---

[9] Robert Rollock, *Select Works of Robert Rollock*, vol. 1, (Edinburgh: Alex Walker, 1849), 469.

The Father, in mercy, comes to us in his Son. Look to where he dwells. Look to the place where he communes with his people. Look to the preaching of the Word, where Christ's mercy is proclaimed. The preaching of the gospel is a means of applying God's promises of mercy to you. When the Word of God is preached by a lawful minister, it is as if Christ himself speaks to you. Consider also the sacraments, the visible signs of God's mercy. Think on your baptism, the sign and seal of your entrance into the covenant of Christ. Reflect upon the Lord's Supper, where the tokens of mercy are given to you by Christ's ministers—bread and wine, signs of his broken body and shed blood.

God manifests his presence now, not in the tabernacle or temple, but in the preaching of his Word and in the administration of his sacraments. And as you come, you come to the place of his continual intercession, to the throne of his mercy, to Christ the King, who reigns in holiness and grace.

Is this not a great motive to come boldly? Heaven is opened to you, a far more glorious place than any earthly type. The throne of mercy stands open, beckoning you to come. Understanding this mercy seat is a grand motive to grow in holiness, that we may be fit to enter into Christ's presence and seek him in all times of need. You do this by faith and repentance—the two graces that flow from the throne to draw you to the throne.

By faith, you look to the Spirit to apply the blood of Christ to cleanse you from all sin (1 John 1:7). By repentance, you put sin to death, that you may serve the living God.

An Appeal to Sinners

But I must appeal to those who do not know Christ—you are enemies of the majesty of God. You are enemies of Christ, and you know it, and *he knows it*. You ought to praise God that you are not already cut off, that you are not already among the damned.

If you have any love for your own soul, turn now. Do not venture another step in rebellion against Christ, lest he tear you in pieces and none deliver you. There is none who can save you apart from him. There is no one who can stand against the Almighty. He will have his justice. He will execute his wrath.

God's counsel to you is this: "Kiss the Son, lest he be angry, and ye perish from the way, when his wrath is kindled but a little," (Psalm 2:12). You will be blessed if you trust in him. And even now, Christ stands ready to treat you with grace from his mercy seat, from his throne of holiness. But if you delay, if you tarry, the time will come when that mercy seat will turn to a throne of judgment.

The Urgency of Pardon

There is a great need for pardon. Nothing else will help you stand when you appear before the great Judge, except the holiness of Christ. You will stand before the holiness of Christ, but if you lack his righteousness, that holiness will be unbearable. He is a consuming fire.

There will be no plea of ignorance. The law has been known. There will be no appeals for mercy, for mercy will have passed. The Judge will open his mercy seat to you, not as a place of grace, but as a place of judgment. The law will stare you in the face, bold and unrelenting, and it will convict you at every turn.

And on that day, there will be no more hope. There will be no wrong verdict. There will be no advocate standing on your behalf. You will stand before the Judge, without a covering, and the sentence will be eternal.

The greatest tragedy in all of history is for a man to leave this world without faith in Christ, without the pardon of his sins, without the covering of the blood of the everlasting covenant.

"What will you do in that day?" What will you do, you who are without Christ? What will you do, you who have rejected his mercy? You will wail. You will wish you had never been born. You will beg the mountains to fall on you to escape the wrath of the Lamb. But there is a way of escape. There is a place of refuge. There is a mercy seat where grace may be found.

Come to the throne of Christ. Come to the mercy seat of the One who dwells between the cherubim. His blood is sufficient to cover you. His mercy is abundant to cleanse you. But do not delay, for the time will come when that seat of mercy will become a seat of judgment, and then it will be too late.

Chapter 6: The Glory

The writer of Hebrews gives us a description of the holiest place, the inner sanctuary of the tabernacle, where the presence of God was manifest:

"And after the second veil, the tabernacle which is called the Holiest of all; Which had the golden censer, and the ark of the covenant overlaid round about with gold, wherein was the golden pot that had manna, and Aaron's rod that budded, and the tables of the covenant; and over it the cherubims of glory shadowing the mercyseat; of which we cannot now speak particularly," (Hebrews 9:3-5).

This passage echoes the original instructions given to Moses: "And thou shalt make two cherubims of gold, of beaten work shalt thou make them, in the two ends of the mercy seat. And make one cherub on the one end, and the other cherub on the other end: even of the mercy seat shall ye make the cherubims on the two ends thereof. And the cherubims shall stretch forth their wings on high, covering the mercy seat with their wings, and their faces shall look one to another; toward the mercy seat shall the faces of the cherubims be. And thou shalt put the mercy seat above upon the ark; and in the ark thou shalt put the testimony that I shall give thee. And there I will meet with thee, and I will commune with thee from above the mercy seat, from between the two cherubims which are upon the ark of the testimony, of all things which I will give thee in commandment unto the children of Israel," (Exodus 25:18-22).

Behind the second curtain lay the holy of holies, the place of ultimate sacredness. Here stood the ark of the covenant, the sacred chest overlaid with gold, containing the three most significant elements of Israel's history and faith:

1. **The tables of the Law** – The very commandments given by God to Moses, a reminder of the covenant and its demands.
2. **Aaron's rod that budded** – A sign of God's chosen leadership and the resurrection power of divine election.
3. **The golden pot of manna** – The provision of God, sustaining his people in the wilderness.

These items rested beneath the mercy seat, the golden covering of the ark, over which the presence of God hovered in the shekinah glory. This earthly throne, crafted by human hands at God's command, was a reflection of the divine reality in heaven.

The Mercy Seat: The Crown of the Ark

Atop the ark was the mercy seat, the place where God communed with his people. It was the place of appeasement, the place of expiation, where sin was dealt with by blood atonement. The Lord declared its purpose: "There I will meet with thee, and I will commune with thee, from above the mercy-seat," (Exodus 25:22). This was the place of divine conversation, the dwelling place of God's presence, the seat where he ruled in holiness and grace.

The Cherubim: Guardians of the Holy Presence

The cherubim were positioned over the mercy seat, overshadowing it with their wings. Their purpose was both symbolic and functional. These angelic figures were guardians of divine glory, warriors of God's holiness.

The first time we encounter cherubim in Scripture is in Genesis: "So he drove out the man; and he placed at the east of the garden of Eden Cherubims, and a flaming sword which turned every way, to keep the way of the tree of life," (Genesis 3:24). They stood as sentinels, barring the way back into the garden for fallen mankind. No one could re-enter paradise without passing the fiery judgment of these angelic beings. This was their function: to stand in the presence of holiness, ensuring that nothing unclean approached.

The cherubim also played a role in the tabernacle and temple:
- Their images were woven into the fabric of the tabernacle curtains.
- They were carved into Solomon's temple, where they spread their wings over the ark (1 Kings 6:23-28).
- They formed the chariot of God, for the Lord is said to ride upon them:

"And he rode upon a cherub, and did fly: yea, he did fly upon the wings of the wind," (Psalm 18:10). The writer of Hebrews ties all of this together: "And over it the cherubims of glory shadowing the mercyseat," (Hebrews 9:5). These angelic beings were more than decoration; they were witnesses of divine majesty, symbols of the heavenly court, signifying that the King of Glory was present.

The cherubim's role in guarding holiness is inseparable from the *function* of the mercy seat. The Lord spoke from between them (Numbers 7:89). The glory cloud of God's presence rested above them (Leviticus 16:2). The mercy seat was his throne, the meeting place of heaven and earth. And yet, this throne was not merely a seat of judgment—it was also a throne of grace. Christ himself is described in this way: "Whom God hath set forth to be a propitiation [ἱλαστήριον, *hilasterion*] through faith in his blood," (Romans 3:25). The Greek word for propitiation is the same word used for the mercy seat. Christ is our mercy seat, the place where atonement is made. The cherubim, who once barred sinful men from God's presence, now bow before the One who made peace by the blood of his cross. The throne of God, attended by cherubim, once meant fiery judgment for fallen men. Now, through Christ, it is a throne of grace, where sinners may come boldly (Hebrews 4:16).

The Cloud of Glory: The Presence of God

Above the mercy seat, the shekinah glory of God rested: "For I will appear in the cloud upon the mercy seat,"

(Leviticus 16:2). This glory cloud was the visible sign of God's presence, the radiance of divine holiness. It was the same cloud that led Israel in the wilderness, the same cloud that descended on Sinai, the same glory that filled the temple at its dedication (2 Chronicles 7:1-2). Yet, in the New Testament, we see this glory manifested in Jesus Christ: "And the Word was made flesh, and dwelt [literally *tabernacled*] among us, and we beheld his glory," (John 1:14). The glory cloud of the Old Testament rested upon the mercy seat. Now, the glory of God dwells in Christ, and through him, in us.

The mercy seat, attended by cherubim, overshadowed by God's glory, was the throne of divine presence. It was there that atonement was made, there that God met with his people, there that justice and mercy were joined together. And all of it pointed to Christ.

- He is the **true Ark of the Covenant**, containing the law, the priestly rod, and the bread of heaven.
- He is the **true Mercy Seat**, the place where atonement is made.
- He is the **true Glory of God**, the radiance of divine presence.
- He is the **true Chariot Throne**, reigning as King in holiness.

Where once the cherubim barred sinners from paradise, now they stand in awe before the Lamb. Where once the mercy seat was hidden behind a veil, now it stands open for all who come through Christ.

Chapter 6: The Glory

Here, at this mercy seat, is grace to help in time of need. Here, at this throne, is mercy for those who boldly come. And here, between the cherubim, sits the King of Glory, reigning forever.

The doctrine that emerges from the text is clear: *the glory of God is the highest end to which all things are subordinate, including the promotion of holiness and the production of happiness.* The divine essence, the dwelling of God, his presence, and his glory are preeminent above all things. Moses understood this when he pleaded with God in Exodus 33:18, "Shew me thy glory." The greatest desire of the righteous is to behold the glory of God, for in it, they find holiness, communion, and ultimate fulfillment.

Christ himself is the manifestation of this glory. John declares, "We saw his glory," (John 1:14). This is not simply a reflection or an emanation, but the direct revelation of divine majesty. The glory of God was visibly demonstrated in the Old Testament through the shekinah presence above the mercy seat, filling the temple with light and splendor. "The glory of the Lord filled the house of the Lord," (2 Kings 8:11). This glory was not merely symbolic but a real and tangible sign of God's dwelling with his people. Christ, in his first coming, revealed the glory of God in his incarnation, and he will return in that same glory: "And then shall they see the Son of man coming in a cloud with power and great glory," (Luke 21:27).

God does all things for his own glory. The final cause of all divine purposes is to magnify himself. Revelation 4:11 states, "Thou art worthy, O Lord, to receive glory, and honour, and power: for thou hast created all things, and for thy pleasure they are and were created." All things exist for God, through God, and unto God. This is the chief end of all creation and of man himself—to glorify God and enjoy him forever. The Lord repeatedly affirms his determination to make his glory known: "As truly as I live, all the earth shall be filled with the glory of the Lord," (Numbers 14:21). The prophet Isaiah records God's own words, "For mine own sake, even for mine own sake, will I do it; for how should my name be polluted? and I will not give my glory unto another," (Isaiah 48:11). In Ezekiel, the Lord declares, "I wrought for my name's sake, that it should not be polluted before the heathen," (Ezekiel 20:9). The glory of God is at the center of all his works, including redemption. Paul teaches that salvation itself is designed to reveal divine glory: "That no flesh should glory in his presence...He that glorieth, let him glory in the Lord," (1 Corinthians 1:26-31).

The decrees of God, the works of God, are all part of one grand and singular purpose—to display his glory. The Westminster Confession of Faith makes this explicit: "God, from all eternity, did, by the most wise and holy counsel of his own will, freely, and unchangeably ordain whatsoever comes to pass."[10] Nothing happens apart from God's set purpose to magnify his name. All things, including salvation and reprobation, providence and judgment, exist for the

---

[10] *1647 Westminster Confession of Faith* 3:1; Psalm 33:11; Ephesians 1:11; Hebrews 6:17.

demonstration of divine glory. "He decrees everything for the manifestation of his glory."[11]

The Sum of Saving Knowledge states, "God decrees for his glory whatsoever comes to pass." The Confession further affirms that he executes his decrees "for the glory of His sovereign power," (WCF 3:7). Every divine action, whether in creation, providence, redemption, or judgment, is an exhibition of his glory. Whether parting the Red Sea, numbering the hairs on a person's head, or dwelling between the cherubim, all of God's works are designed to magnify his presence, his majesty, and the weight of his being.

If God is always working toward the display of his glory, what does that reveal about his intentions? In the eternal counsel of his will, he has determined to seek every means possible to promote his own glory. This endeavor cannot be frustrated. He cannot will anything that he does not ordain to do. Everything he ordains serves to promote the revelation of his divine attributes, whether his holiness, his justice, his mercy, or his love. But above all, God will never fail in attaining the exaltation of his own glory. If he were to fall short in this, he would cease to be God.

The religious worship of God is called *glory*. Paul makes this point in Romans 1:23, stating that fallen men "turned the glory of the incorruptible God, into the similitude of corruptible man." That is, they took what was meant to be pure and heavenly, the worship of the living

---

[11] *1647 Westminster Confession of Faith* 3:3.

God, and perverted it into the worship of created things. Worship is the acknowledgement of God's weightiness, his majesty, and his presence. Because of this, religious worship belongs to God alone. He allows no one to claim his glory for themselves, nor does he permit worship to be given to false gods, to statues, or to idols. To do so is to exchange the truth of God for a lie.

God's people are especially called to worship him in holiness. True worship consists of repentance, faith, and love, and it is only acceptable to God through Christ. Even in their imperfection, when believers worship rightly, God pardons them, sanctifies their service, and enables them to exercise holiness by the Spirit. The psalmist declares, "Give unto the Lord the glory due unto his name; worship the Lord in the beauty of holiness," (Psalm 29:2). The beauty of holiness adorns all true worship, setting it apart from the empty, worldly ways men seek to approach God. Worship must be offered with high thoughts of God's majesty, for the power of godliness is found in reverent adoration. Who would dare to think of God lightly? The presence of Christ, who dwells between the cherubim, is a fearful and weighty thing. Yet many today treat him as if he were a mere friend, a personal companion without sovereign majesty. True worship does not lower Christ to the level of a human friend, but exalts him as the glorious Redeemer and King.

The cherubim, closely associated with God's glory, are honored in this sense but are never to be worshiped. Christians may love and reverence all things God has sanctified for holy use—whether the Ark of the Covenant in the Old Testament or the sacraments under the New—but adoration belongs to God alone. Matthew 4:10 commands, "Thou shalt worship the Lord thy God, and him only shalt thou serve." Even when Cornelius fell at Peter's feet, Peter rebuked him (Acts 10:25). The angel in Revelation did the same to John when he attempted to worship him (Revelation 22:9). Paul and Barnabas stopped the people of Lystra from sacrificing to them (Acts 14:14). True worship acknowledges God's presence alone, giving him the glory due his name.

God's mercy is also called glory. As God is glorious and worship is given for his glory, so too the work of the Gospel is an exhibition of his glory, seen most vividly in his covenant mercy. The biblical concept of covenant is one of war, of conflict, of cutting and sacrifice. Blood is sprinkled on the mercy seat, the throne where God dwells in his glory. Death and life surround the covenant—death for those who are unworthy, life for those redeemed by grace. The Most Holy Place, where the Ark of the Covenant sat, was a chamber of presence, a chamber of holiness, a chamber of death, and a chamber of life.

God's mercy, revealed in Christ, is the perfect righteousness that is freely imputed to sinners for his glory. Isaiah prophesied, "The glory of the Lord shall be revealed," (Isaiah 40:5). Paul echoes this truth, stating, "For all have sinned, and come short of the glory of God," (Romans 3:23). Sinners have fallen from glory, but through mercy, they are restored to it. When the redeemed glory in Christ, they are reflecting his glory back to him. Paul captures this beautifully in Romans 9:22-23: "What if God, willing to shew his wrath, and to make his power known, endured with much longsuffering the vessels of wrath fitted to destruction: and that he might make known the riches of his glory on the vessels of mercy, which he had afore prepared unto glory." God displays his glory in judgment, but more magnificently in mercy. Those he calls his own are made vessels of mercy, prepared to dwell in his presence and partake in his glory.

Christ himself, seated upon his chariot throne, is *the* mercy seat, the very meeting place between God and man. Angels attend him, accompanying his reign, his war against darkness, and his triumph over sin. The glory of God, his weightiness, his majesty, his holiness—all are seen most fully in the work of mercy that flows from his throne. In this, the law and the Gospel are both upheld. The law demonstrates the glory of his justice. The Gospel magnifies the glory of his mercy. The King reigns in holiness, attended by angels, glorified by the incessant cries of worship from the seraphim. It is no wonder that sacrifice is given in blood, for the battle between light and darkness is fierce. The mercy seat, the Ark, the law within, the glory above—all testify to the majesty of Christ.

God delights to display his glory for the good of his people. From the beginning, he maintained covenant communion with Adam, setting him in glorious fellowship with his Creator. Though Adam broke that fellowship, seeking a shortcut to divine wisdom, God in Christ restores it. In Christ, mercy shines brighter than ever before. The goodness of God triumphs over the worst of man's wickedness. The Gospel proclaims that God does good to his greatest enemies, reversing the fall, showing grace to the undeserving, and placing Christ upon the throne of mercy. The Ark is his footstool; the law lies beneath him, satisfied in his perfect obedience. Mercy and justice meet in him. "But God commendeth his love toward us, in that, while we were yet sinners, Christ died for us," (Romans 5:8). Those who come to him find mercy in the chamber of glory, the throne of grace.

As Richard Sibbes rightly says, "The greatest glory of mercy, and love, shining forth to fallen man in Christ, than ever to Adam in innocence."[12] In Christ, the mercy seat becomes the throne of grace, where all may come boldly, covered by the blood of the covenant. The law and the Gospel are united in him—the law displaying the glory of his justice, the Gospel revealing the glory of his mercy. Christ reigns in holiness, attended by angels, glorified by the worship of saints, distributing mercy to all who come in faith. This is the glory of God: his justice, his holiness, his mercy, and his love, all revealed in the person and work of Jesus Christ, the King who reigns upon the throne of grace. Eternal life and happiness consist in the participation of God's glory. Christ himself declared this when he asked, "Ought not Christ to have suffered these things, and to enter into his glory?" (Luke 24:26). The Christian hope rests upon the *promise* of this glory, as Paul affirms: "By whom also we

---

[12] Richard Sibbes, *The Excellency of the Gospel Above the Law*, (London: Tho. Cotes and John Dawson, 1639), 244.

have access by faith into this grace wherein we stand, and rejoice in hope of the glory of God," (Rom. 5:2).

In heaven, God will be seen. The saints are assured of this by the testimony of Scripture. Though in this present state, the physical and fallen bodies of believers lack the capacity to see God, they will be changed. However, even without their glorified bodies, the saints in heaven are beholding him even now. As Paul states, "We are confident, I say, and willing rather to be absent from the body, and to be present with the Lord," (2 Cor. 5:6-8). Their sight is not one of mere faith but of *unhindered apprehension by the faculties of the perfect mind*.

Heaven is the place where God has chosen to most fully reveal himself. This does not imply that he becomes visible in the material sense, but that his *manifestation* there is complete. Heaven is not merely a location; it is where God is fully present in his unveiled glory. There, John the Apostle beheld the throne, the mercy seat, the cherubim, and the Lamb slain before the foundation of the world. The Lamb is the focal point of heavenly worship because, "in Him dwelleth all the fullness of the Godhead bodily," (Col. 2:9). The temple, tabernacle, and mercy seat were all shadows pointing to this perfect reality. When Christians see Christ, they see the Father, for, "he that hath seen me hath seen the Father," (John 14:9).

Seeing Christ is the same as seeing the Father. Jesus is the joy, the vision, the object of the saints' desire. Seeing him prompts eternal praise because, in him, they behold God. Heaven is wonderful because it is an intellectual, emotional, and material sight of God in Jesus Christ, who sits enthroned between the cherubim.

This mercy seat, this ark of the covenant, is called the great white throne. It is a seat of majesty and holiness, described as "white" for its purity and justice. It is a tribunal seat, a throne of judgment or mercy, depending on the standing of the one who approaches. What did John see in Revelation 20? Hebrews already tells us: the bloodied Lamb in all his glory, seated above the cherubim. His presence is both dreadful and glorious.

John records: "And I saw a great white throne, and him that sat on it, from whose face the earth and the heaven fled away; and there was found no place for them. And I saw the dead, small and great, stand before God; and the books were opened: and another book was opened, which is the book of life: and the dead were judged out of those things which were written in the books, according to their works. And the sea gave up the dead which were in it; and death and hell delivered up the dead which were in them: and they were judged every man according to their works. And death and hell were cast into the lake of fire. This is the second death. And whosoever was not found written in the book of life was cast into the lake of fire," (Rev. 20:11-15).

If their names are found written in the book of life, mercy has been extended to them. The great white throne becomes a seat of mercy, the righteousness of Christ in heaven exhibiting all glory in salvation. But if their names are not found written in the book of life, the throne of mercy transforms into a throne of judgment. The holiness of God without protection becomes an unbearable weight, a consuming fire. The rock of judgment crushes them, and they are found wanting. They are cast headlong into hell, where they must suffer eternally under the full weight of God's presence with no covering, for there is no mercy in hell.

All these things tend to the glory of God, the presence of God, the *weightiness* of his presence. His being tends to this as the most amiable being ever to exist in holiness, where angels and men made new proclaim it. His worship tends to it, that all true and sincere worship, prescribed by him, for the good of redeemed men, look to bring glory to God as they experience the presence of God. His covenant tends to it, that by Christ, and Christ alone, his Gospel, that he reigns, successfully accomplishes all he intended in it for his glory to save wicked men by the redemption brought by the blood of the everlasting covenant. His heaven demonstrates it, without hindrance, that his glory may be known to vessels of mercy for all eternity, and that his glory may be known to the vessels of wrath in his justice for all eternity.

The glory of God is the end to which the promotion of holiness, and the production of happiness, and all other ends are subordinate. This is why the ark is what it is and the mercy seat is what it is, and the holiest of holy places is what it is. All of this tends to the glorification of God in Christ.

All Out for the Glory of God

It is the sad estate of professing Christians to use Christian language without ever really understanding what the Christian life is about. What *is* a Christian? What is it to be *almost* a Christian? It is to be at the door, but still outside, not seeing his glory. It is to be educated in a Christian way, without understanding his glory. It is to be connected with a Christian Church, but never really participating in his glory.

(I give a few paraphrased and shortened ideas that Matthew Mead lists in his work, *Almost a Christian*.) A person may have great and eminent gifts, yes, spiritual gifts, and yet be but almost a Christian. Jesus says many people before his great white throne will say, "Did we not do such and such in your name?" People may have a very high profession of religion, doing many external duties of godliness, and yet be but almost a Christian. Did not the Scribes outdo many professing Christians today as it stands in external duties? Such people may go far in opposing their sin, even. A man may hate sin, and yet be almost a Christian; but they will not hate all their sin. Absalom hated Amnon's uncleanness with his sister Tamar. His hatred was so great, that he killed him for it; and yet Absalom was a wicked man, was he not? And yet he hated some sin. People may hate sins that detract from their livelihood, like theft, or from their worldly purity, like rape, and struggle against it, and speak against it, and yet not be a Christian.

People in Christian churches all over the world may make great promises and vows in religion; be very resolved in a good many biblical things, even have resolutions against certain sins, and yet be but almost a Christian. They may struggle with some sin—drunkenness, fornication, adultery, pedophilia, hatred, coveting—in themselves, and yet be but almost a Christian. Oftentimes, most people have great hopes of getting into heaven, great hopes of being saved, and yet be but almost a Christian. They may be very zealous in matters of religion, and yet be but almost a Christian. They may be much in prayer; much in tithing, much in helping the poor, much in study, like the Pharisees were. He may even suffer for Christ in some ways, giving of his things to the poor in Christ's name, and yet be but almost a Christian.

People may have faith, and yet be but *almost* a Christian, like the worldly faith of those which were seeds in the stony ground, that only sprouted for a time. Ten years, twenty—many have that kind of spurious faith for a very long time, but did not yield any fruit. Professing Christians often have a love for the people of God, and they may be but almost a Christian. Potiphar loved Joseph for a time. The wicked may love the righteous for certain reasons. They may do much as it pertains to external duties and outward worship, many things that a true Christian can; and, yet still be but almost a Christian.

A person may have the Spirit of God, and yet be but *almost* a Christian. Like Balaam, who had the Spirit. Like Judas, who exercised a powerful preaching ministry with the other disciples in the Spirit. Like King Saul, who had the Spirit, and yet, when times became hard, he fled to the help of a witch. None of these were in a converting way, but only in externals. Men can be endowed and gifted by the Spirit in a great many things, like Mozart in music, and yet be heinous individuals.

What is a Christian? One whom Christ has received *at his mercy seat*; one whom he has received into his glorious presence and who experiences his glory in holiness. One whom the King has made a new creature. One whom the Redeemer has exercised his mercy in a fall-reversing power of fundamental change. Such are thoroughly convinced of their sin and fallenness. Such are truly united to Christ by mercy. Such that under the blood of sprinkling are instated in the covenant of grace. These are those who have received Christ in return—who now belong to Christ, exercising themselves in sincerity to the chief end of all living things.

Then here is the rub of it all. One who is like Christ is sold out for their chief end, which is the glory of God. One who serves Christ in exemplifying his glory in holiness. John Flavel said, "Rom. 14:8, 'None of us liveth to himself, and no man dyeth to himself, but whether we live, we live to the Lord; and whether we die, we die to the Lord: so then whether we live or die, we are the Lord's.' This is to be a Christian indeed. What is a Christian, but a holy dedicated thing to the Lord? And what greater evidence can there be that Christ set himself apart for you, than your setting yourselves apart for him?"[13]

---

[13] John Flavel, *The Fountain of Life Opened* (London: Printed for Rob. White, for Francis Tyton, 1673), 76.

What is a Christian life but a continual meditation on Christ's mercy, as found at the throne of grace, which they come boldly to, which in turn is the mercy seat, and the throne of his presence, and the throne of his glory, the great white pure perfect righteousness or rightness of Christ's glory? It is a life lived in true repentance, exercised in faith, keeping of a good conscience, and so it cannot go astray for it has been made new by the fall-reversing power of Jesus Christ. This is why the catechism says that the chief end of man is to glorify God and enjoy him forever. They are joined together, because Christ's word places them as a chief end with a subordinate end; the chief end is God's glory, the subordinate end is your happiness.

God put men into a natural desire after happiness. Men have sought out evil to satisfy them since the fall. But Christ's mercy seat is a place that men are changed to rectify rebellion and their criminal behavior. Christ's glory quickens men by a promise of happiness. And men are unable to seek God's glory without seeking their own salvation. As if Christ speaks from between the cherubim, "You desire to be happy, and happiness comes from dwelling in and with me, for I alone am the only adequate Object of true and lasting happiness. And if you truly desire to glorify me, in it you will be happy. Take my honor upon you in all things, and I will secure your eternal happiness in the everlasting covenant."

And so the King changes men, to see and understand those words, and by his glory, his mercy, from his throne of glory, from his dwelling presence in Christ, the mercy seat,

God gives you the ability by the inward change to glorify him and seek his glory above all things, to become one now in his service, instead of those like the Pharisees who loved their kingdom more than God's. Christians seek Christ's glory by mercy, and find in doing so, there are benefits in being happy.

In such glorifying of God, you long to worship him in holiness if you are a Christian. You long to reach heaven, that you might do this forever. The beatific vision is one of the most important ideas you can ponder in this life and the life to come. Sadly, because of the fall and sin, it is by degree that people come to see God. But the most important of all things in life is the gainful perception of Christ that most glorifies God.

See again, is this not the chief end of man, to glorify God and enjoy him forever? This is to perceive God in his glorious character most precisely and have a heart that longs after the experience of knowing him intimately. But it is all by an order of degrees. You first glorify God. Then second, you perceive something of Christ in that action and experience it as the beauty of holiness, and benefit from it. God first, man second. Yet, man is most blessed in the second.

So, *holiness* is found *under* the mercy seat. It is there that Christ's glory is found. In his word, in his power, in his sustenance, in his mercy, at his throne, by his presence, in his dwelling by communion with you. Because in this alone, the glory of God in Jesus Christ is the end to which the promotion of their holiness, and the production of their happiness, and all other ends are subordinate to bringing glory to God, being conformed to Christ, and yet, their happiness is a benefit and profit of consequences of such actions. Next, we will consider in relation to the glory of God, and the mercy of Christ, the atonement of Christ given as both King and Savior.

Chapter 7: The Atonement

Romans 5:11, "And not only so, but we also joy in God through our Lord Jesus Christ, by whom we have now received the atonement."

The word for *atonement* here is taken synecdochically for all of Christ's work that results in criminals being reconciled to the Father—criminals being imperfect people. So, the word is rendered as *reconciliation* in other places, such as 2 Corinthians 5:18-19 and even Romans 5:10, the previous verse, "For if, when we were enemies, we were reconciled to God by the death of his Son, much more, being reconciled, we shall be saved by his life," (Rom. 5:10).

Atonement in the Old Testament was *typical* or Mosaical under the Law and made for sin, as Exodus 29:36 states, "And thou shalt offer every day a bullock for a sin offering for atonement," and again in Exodus 29:37, "Seven days thou shalt make an atonement for the altar, and sanctify it." Exodus 30:16 also speaks of atonement being made "for your souls." When atonement was made by the High Priest for the people, every sin was forgiven, whatever that sin was, "And the priest shall make an atonement for him before the LORD: and it shall be forgiven him for any thing of all that he hath done in trespassing therein," (Lev. 6:7).

As has been the case throughout this study, taking Old Testament pictures and shining the light of Christ upon them to show them as *types* of Christ, atonement in the New Testament is evangelical, under the Gospel, made by Christ the High Priest once for all, which is the argument of Hebrews 9:28 and 10:12-14.[14]

To make atonement is to declare one to be purged from their sins and reconciled to God; reconciliation *presupposes* enmity. The Priest shall make atonement, as it was under ceremonies that touched on that which was fleshly, looking forward to Christ. The blood of bulls and goats under the Old Testament were offered in atonement, in reconciliation, year to year, day to day, for sin, to be a remembrance of sin, to be a remembrance of covenant breaking (original and actual). "But in those sacrifices there is a remembrance again made of sins every year. For it is not possible that the blood of bulls and of goats should take away sins," (Heb. 10:3-4).

The apostle in Romans takes the idea of reconciliation and atonement as the fulfillment of the entire ceremonial system, which looked to Christ by type. Blood was sprinkled by the High Priest in the holiest of holy places, upon and before the holy things of God, the ark of his covenant, that he would forgive sins and make reconciliation. Such an act was done in monotony, but necessarily; lots of sins, lots of sacrifices.

The death and whole sufferings of the Christ who came—one part of his sufferings is put for the entirety of it.

---

[14] Not to confuse you, the sum and substance of the Covenant of Faith is always evangelical in *any* testament. In the old or new, the Covenant of Faith at its core is *evangelical*.

Ephesians 1:7, "By whom we have redemption through his blood." This idea is often used throughout Romans and Hebrews and throughout Paul's epistles. The blood of Christ (one part of his sufferings) is put synecdochically for the whole sufferings—visible and invisible—of all his work and merit, including his cross, the entirety of the "how" of the Gospel. It would be a theological mistake to consider only his physical sufferings as sufficient without the entirety of the spiritual blessing of the Father in his covenant work with the Son, being executed by divine decree to save his people and all that it entails, which includes physical suffering. These Old Testament sacrifices and the sprinkling of blood, the death of cruelty of death in slaying beasts for atonement, for mediation, typified the bloody sacrifice of Christ in his death. This is why the New Testament is filled with ideas of being plunged beneath the blood of Christ, sprinkled with the blood of Christ, dipped in the blood of Christ, covered in the blood of Christ.

In the blood of the covenant, the blood of beasts sacrificed under the Law was a sign and pledge of the old way of the *covenant of grace*, which was administered in figures and types—arks and bread, rods and mercy seats, crowns and gold—all prefiguring Christ (*i.e.* evangelical salvation). Such sacrifices were attached to the throne of mercy, to the throne of grace, where blood was sprinkled for cleansing. It was this way for divine justice to enact righteously against the wickedness of criminals against the glory of the Father. Justice must be exercised by God against sin, and mercy must be given to the sinner so that the sinner may then be able to repent and walk justly. For this to occur, an atonement must be made to divine justice by some go-between that God accepts. This is called a Surety, and then the Father will mercifully pardon all those for whom the Surety gives its life. Through the mercy of the Father, men may be forgiven and exempt from punishment by the substitution of a surety in their stead. From the beginning, it was this way, "Unto Adam also and to his wife did the LORD God make coats of skins, and clothed them," (Gen. 3:21). Why did he do this? Even at the first sin, the Lord killed the animals instead of killing the rebels. The animals were a substitution for them right from the very start.

All Old Testament sacrifices are object lessons for sinners who see and understand the lesson of atonement or reconciliation with the Father. The ground of these types and their effectiveness is the substitutionary atonement of Christ for them; his work, death, and merit uphold all types gone before him. The One who makes atonement must be able to make a payment for the debt. It is an infinite debt. It is an affront to infinite holiness. It is an affront to God's infinite character and infinite law.

The blood of Christ, by which the new covenant is ratified, upholds all spiritual designs which went before. The blood of Christ, by which God the Father had agreed and promised to save his people from their sins, for his wrath is against sin; and for which they promise forever to serve him.

When this blood was sprinkled on the ark of the covenant, the ark of the covenant of grace, such sprinkling gave force and power to the blood of Christ from his Godhead for purging of sins (Lev. 1:5, 11, 15; 1 Peter 1:2; Acts 20:28; 2 Cor. 5:18-19). Such is called the *blood of sprinkling*, now seen in the blood of Jesus shed in his cruel death, by which the hearts of the faithful, being sprinkled and who believe on him through faith, their sins are washed away, that they may be accepted of God, Heb. 12:24, "to the blood of sprinkling." This is the blood of the atonement, the blood of the covenant. Being a death in covenant, the death and blood-shedding of Christ joined with his Father's curse, by which the Testament or covenant of salvation was ratified, Heb. 10:29, "and count the blood of the testament."

The believer has received the atonement. Paul, speaking of the atonement, no doubt brings in the fulfilling completion of Christ's work as it was typified by the atonement day in the Old Testament. The Day of Atonement was intended to stop catastrophes like Nadab and Abihu being slain while making atonement, if people would follow what God has prescribed.

They did this for atonement year after year under Mosaical legislation. But now, in the sending of the Son of God, all this is *fulfilled* in the work of Christ. He is the blood of sprinkling, he is the atonement, he is the sacrifice, he is the scapegoat, he is the One who dies and takes away sins, not the possibility of atonement, but actual atonement.

And what is the effect of such a thing? "...we also joy in God through our Lord Jesus Christ, by whom we have now received the atonement," (Rom. 5:11). What excellent Scriptural language. Believers do not accept the atonement;

they receive it. And they joy in the Father, through Christ, by whom they have received reconciliation.

Doctrine: *Christians rejoice in the Father through the Lord Jesus because of his atonement, which has reconciled them.*

One might think, how does this relate *to the ark?* I hope this is not unclear—there is a great exchange made here. The ark of the covenant, prefiguring the work of Christ, *is* the Christ in type, the sacrifice, the Law, the Bread of Life, the Resurrection, correction, discipline, guidance, sustenance—to find mercy—where Christ sits and rules from on high upon his mercy seat of glory between the cherubim, dwelling and communing with those who have received the atonement. His work is *effectual.* By way of effect, what he intends in his work is accomplished, which is why there is no question as to whether Christians can come boldly to the throne of grace, where the Old Testament priest could only come once a year. The great exchange of the Father is that he takes the death of his Son for the sinner. Sinners can come to the mercy seat time and time again, looking for grace to help in time of need, where Christ is seated at the right hand of the Father. "It is that God, in the Scripture, upon the death of Christ is said to be reconciled, to be returned to peace with them for whom he so died, the enmity being slain and peace actually made," (Eph. 2:14-16, Col. 1:20).[15]

---

[15] John Owen, *The Works of John Owen,* ed. William H. Goold, vol. 10 (Edinburgh: T&T Clark, n.d.), 459.

And who is this that comes, but Christ's people, who have the blood of sprinkling applied to them? The evangelical church today in the world rejects this notion almost outrightly.

Jesus Christ taught that none are lost for whom he died. What a tragic thing it would be for the Mediator to mediate and make merely a way to escape and save no one—that is the religion of the natural man who wants some part in making atonement and reconciliation. John 6:37-40 says, "All that the Father giveth me shall come to me; and him that cometh to me I will in no wise cast out. For I came down from heaven, not to do mine own will, but the will of him that sent me. And this is the Father's will which hath sent me, that of all which he hath given me I should lose nothing, but should raise it up again at the last day. And this is the will of him that sent me, that every one which seeth the Son, and believeth on him, may have everlasting life: and I will raise him up at the last day." In fact, the angelic proclamation demonstrates that Jesus will complete what he sets out to do, *"And she shall bring forth a son, and thou shalt call his name JESUS: for he shall save his people from their sins,"* (Matt. 1:21). Not that he might, or possibly could, or makes a mere way to do it, but rather, they have received—upon pain of his death, and in his exaltation—the atonement. They receive the atonement. It is placed squarely in their new hearts.

Jesus himself says he dies for his sheep, *"As the Father knoweth me, even so know I the Father: and I lay down my life for the sheep,"* (John 10:15). Jesus does not die for any of the goats. No

Philistine ever participated in the Day of Atonement from a distance, outside the camp. One was in the camp or not. Amorites, Jebusites, Philistines—they received no atonement on the Day of Atonement. Christ lays his life down for his friends, *"Greater love hath no man than this, that a man lay down his life for his friends,"* (John 15:13).

The church itself is bought with his blood—just the church—*"Take heed therefore unto yourselves, and to all the flock, over the which the Holy Ghost hath made you overseers, to feed the church of God, which he hath purchased with his own blood,"* (Acts 20:28). All those who will be in heaven have received the atonement. Paul even remarks that marriage is much like the union between Christ and the church. Christ is married to his bride and gave himself for his bride. *"Husbands, love your wives, even as Christ also loved the church, and gave himself for it,"* (Eph. 5:25).

Christ's death, then, is that substitutionary atonement on behalf of his people. He died to save them, secure them, and bring them to glory; he died in their place because rebels, being sinners, deserve not only death but eternal death. The famed Synod of Dordt said, *"Since, therefore, we are unable to make that satisfaction in our own persons, or to deliver ourselves from the wrath of God, He has been pleased of His infinite mercy to give His only begotten Son for our Surety, who was made sin, and became a curse for us and in our stead, that He might make satisfaction to divine justice on our behalf."*[16]

---

[16] *Canons of Dordt*, 2.2.

For the elect, Christ actually obtained salvation in his atonement, and the Holy Spirit applies that salvation, which the Father first decreed would take place *for* elect sinners. Jesus actually atones for the guilt of his people; it happens when he does it. Jesus said, *"For the Son of Man has come to seek and to save that which was lost,"* (Luke 19:10). Not only does he seek and save, but he also reconciles his people to God, one verse previous to our text, *"For if when we were enemies we were reconciled to God through the death of His Son, much more, having been reconciled, we shall be saved by His life,"* (Rom. 5:10).

It is the pipe dream of *heretics* to say that Christ merely *made a way*; it is the natural man's religion to say so and place the ability or saving factor in one's own hands—it is an affront to Jesus Christ and his Kingship. He did not make a "way of salvation" but obtained salvation for his people, as Hebrews 9:12 makes clear, *"By his own blood he entered in once into the holy place, having obtained eternal redemption for us."* Either he obtained it or he didn't; most of the contemporary church doesn't think he did.

Through the true human nature that the Son assumed to himself, he voluntarily gave himself up as a substitutionary atonement for his people. He stood in their place. This is the whole meaning of being safe in the ark of the covenant. Christ is the ark. In him, there is safety. If God places one in the ark under the mercy seat, they are safe.

Christ did this, halting the Father's wrath from striking his people. He took their sin; he drank the dregs of that cup. In essence, the Son of Man saved his people from himself—from his wrath. This is the hinge of the incarnation—that the Son became flesh and dwelt among us, to give his life as a ransom for many. He took on this human nature so that such a nature could do three things—be humiliated, be perfect in all his works, and be slain as a sacrificial offering to appease the wrath of the Father. With the power to wash his people in the sprinkling of his blood, instead of leaving them in their own filth, he came and lived among the filthy in order to save them.

Jesus was very forthright to declare the mind and intention of the Father, he being God's Divine Messenger and Herald, the Son of Man, the Great Exegete of the Father, to declare him (John 1:18). In his first sermon, if you recall, as with his forerunner John, he preached God's kingdom and repentance; he preached God's gospel. As a reminder, to preach the kingdom involves the King and his will. Christ is the absolute King over the universe, governing everything. He is particular as King in his government of his church. He rules over the fall as King and can reverse the fall. He does this through his covenant. The Father does this through his Mediator of the covenant. He does this through the Christ, who is the divine and all-powerful Son of Man.

For Jesus to preach about the Kingdom is to preach about the ark of the covenant; to preach the kingdom is to preach about entry into the kingdom by atonement. Repentance is in light of the fall, and the waywardness of men in their desire to be rebels instead of servants needs reconciliation. Repentance includes repentance from sin, in light of God's holy law and providence over sinful men. It is an evangelical grace, a supernatural grace, that is required speedily for entrance into the kingdom and for the kingdom to reside in men; it is given by the decree of the Father.

To gain repentance from the King, in his dominion over the fall, is to gain it by the Father's mercy and good pleasure, and in his way, and in no other way. But, to gain such supernatural repentance is only by the substitutionary atonement of his Mediator. It is not possible to gain it in any other way. The Father is the *who* of the gospel, his kingdom is the *what* of the gospel, the fall-reversing power of God in men is the exercise of the *why* of the gospel, and the work and merit of the Christ in his life and atonement and reconciliation (and all things gathered from that idea) is the *how* of all those good tidings that are preached by faithful ministers of the Gospel.

Why do men need atonement? It is because original sin makes men guilty and necessitates punishment because sin is hated by God and is an affront to him. It is a debt that all men are bound to pay to divine justice, as a result of the fall. In this way, the Apostle says, *"even Jesus, which delivered us from the wrath to come,"* (1 Thess. 1:10).

Original sin was reckoned to man's account by God because of Adam's transgression under the *Covenant of Works*. *"...for in the day that thou eatest thereof thou shalt surely die,"* (Gen. 2:17). *"But they like Adam have transgressed the covenant: there have they dealt treacherously against me,"* (Hosea 6:7).

All men are bound up under this terrible plight. Sin is enmity against God, which makes men God-haters at conception, even if they deny it. *"Behold, I was shapen in iniquity; and in sin did my mother conceive me,"* (Psa. 51:5). *"...visiting the iniquity of the fathers upon the children unto the third and fourth generation of them that hate me,"* (Exod. 20:5), God says these things. Sin is a cosmic crime against the Father by God-haters. They need reconciliation because, *"God saw that the wickedness of man was great in the earth, and that every imagination of the thoughts of his heart was only evil continually,"* (Gen. 6:5).

To repent, then, is impossible without God's help because men are stinking dead corpses, dead in sin, and God-haters. Reconciliation is what is needful, and men cannot reconcile themselves. It is impossible without God's saving and renewing hand to save them. *"And I will give them one heart, and I will put a new spirit within you; and I will take the stony heart out of their flesh, and will give them an heart of flesh,"* (Ezek. 11:19). Who does this? God does this.

In order to have the wrath of the Father subsided, and for sin to be reversed in its effect on fallen men, there must be something or someone that goes between the sinner and God. There must be a payment of the debt contracted by sin, the appeasing of divine wrath, and the expiation of guilt. Where is the blood of sprinkling to occur; what shall it hit when it is sprinkled? Because sin is a wage that God will pay in righteousness and justice, *"...the soul that sinneth, it shall die,"* (Ezek. 18:4). What is owed to God is complete perfection in character and conduct. So, appeasing God's wrath against sin must take place; something must satisfy God. And in this satisfaction, God is able to justify sinners who come to him by this satisfaction. *"...by his knowledge shall my righteous servant justify many; for he shall bear their iniquities,"* (Isa. 53:11).

All or many? Jesus knows what he does. This is why when he speaks of communion with his people, he says of the blood of the New Testament, *"For this is my blood of the new testament, which is shed for many for the remission of sins,"* (Matt. 26:28), referencing Isaiah. For those that are intended by it. *"Then will I sprinkle clean water upon you, and ye shall be clean: from all your filthiness, and from all your idols, will I cleanse you,"* (Ezek. 36:25).

God is satisfied in what? A sinner's accepting of Christ as Savior? Nonsense; biblically devoid of any proof. God is satisfied in the work of his Son's atonement, and the Spirit then applies that atonement to his people. *"He shall see of the travail of his soul, and shall be satisfied: by his knowledge shall my righteous servant justify many; for he shall bear their iniquities,"* (Isa. 53:11). What does it mean to bear another's iniquities? Man cannot do it; he's wicked and evil. Someone perfect must do it, in order to satisfy God's justice and appease his wrath. Whoever does this must meet all the requirements of atonement and offer something that will satisfy the Great King who reigns in heaven as the infinite God of righteousness.

The Christ was designated the Mediator, the near Kinsman of his people, to fulfill all the stipulations of the covenant on behalf of those he represented to reconcile them to the Father. Adam represented the *"all"* of humanity. Christ represented the *"all"* of his church, the many, the sheep, his friends. In this, he is both High Priest and sacrifice, to substitute himself in the *"many's"* stead and make atonement by enduring all the requirements of God's law for them. He fulfills all things required by God, and that willingly as God's fellow in covenant with the Father. *"...the man that is my fellow,"* (Zech. 13:7). *"...and this is his name whereby he shall be called, THE LORD OUR RIGHTEOUSNESS,"* (Jer. 23:6). When he completes this, the Father accepts him and all his work of atonement for those he came to save.

Reconciliation is an agreement and atonement with God by dying to take away sin, or by remission of sins through his death, (Heb. 2:17). Here, the ministry of the Gospel, pronouncing and declaring reconciliation with God, by free forgiveness of sins, and justification offered to believers by Christ is the point of the mercy seat of Christ and the atonement of Christ, all for his glory; *"And hath given unto us the ministry of reconciliation,"* (2 Cor. 5:18). Such a word of reconciliation is the message or doctrine of atonement, *"...and hath committed unto us the word of reconciliation,"* (2 Cor. 5:19).

Such people are reconciled by Christ, or they aren't—there is no in-between. Either he restores all former love, concord, and familiarity that was accustomed to be between the Father and his people, or he doesn't. All hatred and discord which set them apart, God has been appeased and satisfied in the atonement of his Son. And in this way, to take grace and favor, such as were enemies through sin, God was in Christ reconciling not just the Jews as the Day of Atonement showed, but the many scattered across the face of the whole world, for all time, to himself.

God is reconciled to man *when*, forgiving his sins, he takes him into his favor, because men are reconciled to God by the blood of sprinkling which the Father accepts in Christ. What sins will the Father hold men accountable for that Christ died for? Are there any? No, not a one. And when dead stinking corpses are brought to life, when they then believe the forgiveness of their sins through Christ, they receive the love and favor of the Father, and they then refrain and abstain from what they can to offend God, (Col. 1:20; 2 Cor. 5:20). A simple way to say this is that Christ made peace between criminals and the Father by atonement. Brought them near, made a union between them. Reconciled to God, restored to his favor, God pacified toward his people.

Christ has redeemed men by the price of his blood. He redeemed men by the blood of the atonement made for them. *"...he is brought as a lamb to the slaughter,"* (Isa. 53:7). *"...I gave my back to the smiters..."* (Isa. 50:6). *"...when thou shalt make his soul an offering for sin,"* (Isa. 53:10). *"...I will save them... wherein they have sinned, and will cleanse them,"* (Ezek. 37:23). *"...to make an atonement for your souls,"* (Exod. 30:15). *"...to make an atonement...,"* (2 Chron. 29:24).

His very name is substitutionary in its work. *"...and with him is plenteous redemption. And he shall redeem Israel from all his iniquities,"* (Psa. 130:7-8). *"...and this is his name whereby he shall be called, THE LORD OUR RIGHTEOUSNESS,"* (Jer. 23:6). All of this is substitutionary language; the Old Testament is a substitutionary testament—but so is the New.

Christ died on behalf of his people to save them and make atonement for them. *"...and to make an end of sins, and to make reconciliation for iniquity, and to bring in everlasting righteousness, and to seal up the vision and prophecy, and to anoint the most Holy,"* (Dan. 9:24). Christ died for his people; he in the place of others. *"...he hath borne our griefs,"* (Isa. 53:4). *"...for the transgression of my people was he stricken,"* (Isa. 53:8). The sins are borne by him being bruised and wounded, sin laid on him as the atoning sacrifice, the scapegoat. He, *"...makes his soul an offering for sin,"* (Isa. 53:10).

He is a priest in all these covenantal acts pertaining to God, to appease him by an atoning sacrifice where he comes into the most holy place, which is heaven, by the blood of sprinkling, to sit on the ark of his testimony, his mercy seat, to find reconciled sinners at his feet seeking him boldly because of his work. *"Even as the Son of man came not to be ministered unto, but to minister, and to give his life a ransom for many,"* (Matt. 20:28). *"But this man, after he had offered one sacrifice for sins for ever, sat down on the right hand of God,"* (Heb. 10:12). Where did he sit but on his mercy seat in the heavenly places. God sending, *"his Son to be the propitiation for our sins,"* (1

John 4:10). "*...even Jesus, which delivered us from the wrath to come,*" (1 Thess. 1:10).

And simply, are Christians not joyful in this? Christians rejoice in the Father, through the Lord Jesus, because of his atonement which has reconciled them; for they received the atonement and received his blessing.

What triumph is there for sinners in Christ's atonement? Christ's exaltation is his current intercession for his *"many"* to whom he has made atonement. The magnificent temple built by Solomon in Jerusalem is called the house and habitation of God, and is metaphorically seen for the heaven of God's glory. Christ is front and center, seated on his throne, between the cherubim, in glory—the glory of his exaltation, the glory of his Father—for the church, to give them joy, found in the most holy place. "*I bring [them] to my holy mountain, and make them joyful in my house of prayer,*" (Isa. 56:7).

Christ is said to be the temple of the elect in heaven, "*And I saw no temple therein: for the Lord God Almighty and the Lamb are the temple of it,*" (Rev. 21:22). The throne to which Christ is front and center for his people is the ark of his testimony, which is no longer a type—the writer of Hebrews has said that his people go boldly to that throne. It is the place of Christ's atonement and the place to find grace and mercy, at the mercy seat. God never does away with these things to make them obsolete—he fulfills them to make them full.

Sacrifice has not been done away with, for Christ is the sacrifice. Atonement is not done away with; the Day of

Atonement is not done away with—it is fulfilled in Christ. The new Testator has come, and all things are new by way of a fulfilled perspective. Should we then prepare a goat or bull? No, those types are fulfilled; they are realized in Christ, abolished physically because of fulfillment, not merely by replacement. To simply replace something is to empty it of its meaning. But there are no more types because types find their fulfillment in Christ. You see, *we will not speak any more, nor remember the ark of the covenant in his day, because he is the ark, he is the mercy seat, he is the bread, the staff, the word, the crown, the glory, and such.* But understand the Old Testament picture, to which you go to the throne of grace to find help in time of need. It is the throne of Christ. It is the ark he sits upon, sprinkled with the blood of the Lamb. Sometimes, words are taken for the whole thing, such as an altar being used to denote the whole mystery of Christ the Mediator. "*We have an altar,*" (Heb. 13:10). And sometimes, even those things have further enlightening meaning—coming to the altar, coming to the throne, coming to the place where Christ dwells in glory.

Oftentimes, divine worship in the New Testament borrows from the ancient rites because they were *types*. For example, "*In that day shall there be an altar to the LORD in the midst of the land of Egypt, and a pillar at the border thereof to the LORD,*" (Isa. 19:19). That is the time of the Gospel, where Christ is our altar. That is the time of the Gospel, where his people go boldly to his throne of grace.

Christ is called *propitiation* (*hilasterion*) in Romans 3:25 because he became the great sacrifice that satisfied for the sins of his people. He is called atonement with respect to the type which he fulfills. In that old temple, God appeared in a cloud and thick darkness, (1 Kings 8:10-12). Paul says of the truth of the New Testament that God is manifest in the flesh—no more clouds of glory. His illustrious manifestation removed the shadow, that obscure dark one of old, now light and bright.

In the old temple, the Mercy Seat was placed upon the Ark of the Covenant in the holy of holies. Of Christ, he is justified in Spirit; when he was risen from the dead and so declared himself the true atonement, having made satisfaction for the sins of the many, and perfectly fulfilled the Divine Law (the Tables of which were contained in the Ark of the Covenant), over which he sits, sitting upon that crown, sitting between the cherubim.

In the old temple, there were cherubim over the Mercy Seat, (Heb. 9:5). Christ was seen of angels, who were glorious and true witnesses of his resurrection and glory, (Matt. 28:2; 1 Peter 1:12). In the old temple, the Jews were taught the doctrine of the Messiah, who was to come. Paul says that Christ was preached to the Gentiles (not to the Jews alone), believed on in the world. *"The sound of the Apostles went out into all the earth,"* (Rom. 10:18), and their doctrine was received by the many, all true believers, (Col. 1:5-6).

In the old temple, the visible appearance of God was not ordinary or perpetual—it was once a year. But Paul says of Christ, having manifested himself in the earth, that he was received up in glory, as if he had said he has withdrawn his visible presence from his church, yet he is gloriously, truly, and invisibly near. For he is *received up in glory*—at the right hand of the Father—present with his people to the end of the world, seated on his seat of mercy, his throne, which sinners may boldly approach.

Christ is a substitution for poor sinners, and poor sinners find acceptance by the Father at the throne of mercy, at the place of the blood of sprinkling. The sacrifice of Christ alone is the only sacrifice, on its own account, acceptable to God that allows sinners entrance into the kingdom—his atonement, his reconciliation of them and the Father. Your heart, as I have said in times past, should be sprinkled under the blood of Christ; soaked in it even. As if you were leaning there, bowed down by the ark of the covenant, where the blood of Christ spilled over onto you, and you can rest there boldly, near his divine presence.

How is man freed from the misery of death and hell and saved? By the Savior, his atonement, where sinners may be sprinkled by the blood of the everlasting covenant. This should be the grounds of eminent joy for you, being sprinkled by the blood of reconciliation. In this substitutionary atonement, he gives you a very special gift. I've called it in the past *the gift of discrimination*. The Gospel is preached indiscriminately, and all who repent and look to the Christ to be saved may be saved. But salvation is also a gift of discrimination—it is for Jacobs, *not Esaus*.

Repentance is given by atonement—that gift, for it is the foundation of salvation in Christ and reconciliation with the Father, is bestowed on the sheep, and they will hear the voice of the shepherd. Repentance makes a discriminating line for you. Either one repents, or they don't. Either one is sprinkled by the blood of Christ, or he isn't. Either one is saved or lost, and repentance is part of the gift of reconciliation.

You must know this substitutionary atonement, according to Romans 5, if you are to be converted and saved. Because when you marry the idea of atonement to the work of atonement laid out in Hebrews, and see the work of Christ in its types fulfilled, these pictures become so much more to you who are saved, and are a means of great comfort. As Christ's substitutionary atonement is once laid out, and repentance is once laid down by mercy—at the altar, at the throne, by the ark, in heaven—it is never done away with, but rather, laid once.

The building of God's people has this atoning foundation in Christ Jesus, and the manner to find grace to help, to find mercy, is through his atonement alone. People do not like this doctrine because they don't like the idea that there are Jacobs and Esaus. There are those God loves, and there are those God hates. They don't like that one son is loved and one son is hated. They don't like what God says because they overlay their emotional response to salvation with their desires and their thoughts of how God *ought* to be, rather than how he *actually* is. It is because they do not understand God, and they do not understand themselves.

In books and sermons I've talked about joy, delight, pleasure, satisfaction in *Christ the Apple Tree*, leaping for joy in the joy of true religion, and such things. To understand that the throne of the King is the place of the highest joy is greatly useful for daily meditation. For when do you have needs? For when do you need grace? For to whom do you turn? Where is the place of turning to? Link such dots together, consider these things over and over, and do not let them slip, for they will bring you great comfort and joy.

When the Apostle says, *"receive the atonement,"* as expressed in Romans 5:11, we receive together with it all the fruits of the atonement—that God may stir us up to understand what a wonder of wonders it is. Your faith in his work comes and brings your soul to Christ as he is lifted up and seated on his throne, but such is always accompanied with love and mercy, by which your soul adheres to Christ when it boldly comes to the place of his blood of sprinkling. Even considering Esther's throne and the golden scepter of the King, those pictures turn more intricate to consider in the throne, add in the ark, and then apply blood.[17]

And does this not cause you great joy of heart, and peace of mind, and comfort and satisfaction? All your faith, whatever can be mustered, whatever you rightly believe, whatever you rightly think, however you cleave to the Lord Jesus is summed up by the Apostle in these words: *"receiving the atonement."* The whole of it is there summed up for you. It does not matter if you are a young Christian or an old Christian, or a preacher, or a theologian, or a disciple, or

---

[17] Many of my past sermons and books deal with Esther's imagery.

what have you. When you think of *receiving the atonement*, it sums up everything you rightly believe in Christ's work.

And when you consider where and how that atonement was made, and how it fulfilled all those parts to God's covenant, and what Christ did with *you* on his mind when dying on the cross, and then *you*, resurrected with him in his resurrection, and now *he*, in heaven, interceding for you in a place where you can boldly come, it is all summed up for you in receiving such an atonement by faith. You believe his words. Your faith is a bestowal of mercy from Christ—a Spirit-given trust on the Son's divine mercy from his throne, believing steadfastly that such blood of sprinkling is to be relied on and is trustworthy. In this, you find *real* joy.

People all over the world believe that such a person as Jesus Christ existed. There are many hardened atheists who believe that there is much evidence for Christ to have existed and walked the earth in his time. Many religious people believe that Christ existed, and they think all they need to do is believe that he came, died on a cross, and even rose from the dead. They think to themselves, *"There is no more I really need to care about than to believe that Christ died for sinners."*

But it does not matter if, like the devil, you believe Jesus existed and walked the earth, and it does not matter that, if like the devil, you believe he died for sinners. There must be something more—some experimental means by which that Christ is made yours. Otherwise, without application of the atonement to you personally, there is no joy to be had in the collection of mere facts.

There must be an effectual application of that atonement and a continued reliance on it—a remembrancer of it. For we read of his blood shed and his blood sprinkled, of *making* the atonement, and as Paul preached, *receiving* the atonement, as our text says. The Father accepts his people for Christ's sake, for his merit and worthiness. But then there is a way the Father appointed how they shall be accepted, without presumption. One cannot *presume* they have received the atonement without an application of it in their lives.

As Thomas Manton says, *"The cup of salvation yields no benefit to us except we drink of it. Therefore since such a great part of the world miscarry, let us see that we do not defraud ourselves of so great a benefit."*[18] Let it not be that you hear about this ark, about this atonement, about this blood of sprinkling, and merely collect it theologically in your mind as a fact, but that you experience the atonement in the work of Christ, by the Spirit in your soul through believing and faith. That you have joy in the triumph of the Christ, and that you have joy in the Father, through the atonement of the Lord Jesus, which has reconciled you forever in his love.

---

[18] Thomas Manton, *The Complete Works of Thomas Manton*, vol. 21 (London: James Nisbet & Co., 1874), 277.

Chapter 8: The Wings

Psalm 61:4, "I will abide in thy tabernacle for ever: I will trust in the covert of thy wings."

The psalm begins with a distressed call for the Lord to hear David's prayer. He desires help—where shall he find it? He seems to be away from the temple, or if this psalm was penned by David after his dealings with Absalom, it is written in light of having been away in the far reaches of the earth, hiding and running. "The end of the earth" is that place which is far away. David is fainting under duress in the context of these words, or when these words were meaningful in action for him. He is sinking, as one sinks in water, and he petitions the throne of grace—God—to put him in a place of safety.

In this psalm, there are three images of safety. It is described in some of the best and well-known images in the Bible of protection. There is *"the rock that is higher than I"* (verse 2). There is *a strong tower* (verse 3), where refuge is found.

With verse 4, David articulates a desire to live in God's tabernacle forever. *Your tent*, he says. Why is this? In God's tabernacle, it is a solid rock, a place of protection, a strong tower—actually, in the way the tabernacle was meant to be constructed, as reaching into the heavens. And in this tower, there is a place where David can find protection, which is described as under the protection of the wings of the cherubim, the winged creatures supporting the

Lord's throne as set on the crown of God's ark, on the mercy seat.

From his prayer to be delivered comes his desire to be always protected by God. He looks to trust in the Almighty and in the place of protection of the Almighty, and where does he choose to go and reside? If evil men are advancing against him, where does he want to go? If his enemies and foes are attacking him, what is the place of refuge?

Certainly, it is to God, but it is in a particular place. He knows that the only refuge of a man in trouble is where the mercy of the Lord will attend him. It does not matter whether he is dealing with sin, or the miseries of this life, or some peril—even at the hand of his own son, Absalom. Whatever that evil is that is advancing against him, in mercy alone can one find protection. There is no relief or assistance in anything else.

David knows that the Lord offers assistance and protection to miserable sinners when the miseries of the evil day come against them. David finds the solace of the everlasting covenant, in the tabernacle, in the holiest of holy places, under the wings of the cherubim, of the stretching of the wings of the cherubim about the mercy seat.

He knows that in the *shadow* of God's wings—not that God has physical wings, but in the similitude of the cherubim on the mercy seat, which he saw when the ark came to rest in Jerusalem—is the *place* of respite and reprieve. It was the place above which God dwells, and the place below which miserable sinners can find assistance.

Grace to help in time of need—boldly so—to go to God's throne of grace. To be placed in the shadow of his wings.
No doubt the hovering idea of the presence of God in the glory cloud above the ark made a shadow by the cherubim's wings, in which humble sinners who are set under the mercy seat could be safe.

Doctrine: *God's love and protection in Christ to sinners is found under the mercy seat.*

Sinners who know they are sinners and have been saved by grace look to God, through Christ, in the power of the Spirit, to keep them safe. They are hidden in Christ. *"...your life is hid with Christ in God,"* (Col. 3:3). Where are they hid? To hide something means to conceal and keep anything from sight and the knowledge of others, that it may be secret and safe.

It can have both negative and positive ideas attached to it. To keep one's sins in silence—either not confessed at all or not confessed genuinely—is negative. *"He that hideth his sins shall not prosper,"* (Prov. 28:13; *cf.* Job 3:33; Psalm 32:3-4). In this way, men hide their sins. But in the positive sense, as considering the mercy seat, it is to cover sin by the free forgiveness of God—not only hiding one's sin in the shadows, but God allowing his face to be kept or hid from such sins. *"Hide thy face from my sins, and blot out all mine iniquities,"* (Psalm 51:9). In this way, God hides sin from his view, *so to speak*—to protect and keep one safe from his dealing with sin, from his *justice toward sin*. *"In time of my troubles he hath hid me,"* (Psalm 27:5). In this way, God hides his people. It is to appeal to God to put one on the rock, in the place of refuge under the promises and protection of God, by a true and sincere faith—repenting of sin and setting oneself in the place of his divine protection, that is, his throne, in the shadows of his wings.

The godly hide themselves under the *wings* of God's mercy seat. To keep out of God's sight, as he would deal with sin in a most terrible fashion if it were exposed, the prophet Habakkuk said he cannot bear to look upon sin—the idea being that sin set in his sight will not cause him to dwell with it. It must be kept secret, and covered, hidden under the place of mercy.

Where are such people hidden but in the shadow of God—(which is metaphorical, for God does not cast a shadow)? The idea of a shadow is taken for a representation of another thing. In this way, the Ceremonial Law was a shadow of the benefits of the Gospel and of the Kingdom of Heaven (Hebrews 8:5, 10; Colossians 2:17). As it pertains to the physical, shadows are cool places, serving for bodily refreshment in a time of great heat. As it applies to the spiritual, sin stirs the wrath of God to a great heat, which is why pictures of hell are of heat, flame, and torment. To reside under the shadow of God's protection is to find refreshment or comfort from God. This may be in light of, after, or in some difficult affliction or great danger. *"He that dwelleth in the secret place of the most High shall abide under the shadow of the Almighty,"* (Psalm 91:1), where, *"He shall cover thee with his feathers, and under his wings shalt thou trust,"* (Psalm 91:4), and *"...for the destruction that wasteth at noonday,"* (Psalm 91:6).

In this way, God's glory is mixed with his mercy seat—a shadow under his wings in respect to his protection and deliverance. *"For thou hast been ... a refuge from the storm, a shadow from the heat,"* (Isaiah 25:4).

Jesus Christ is the Redeemer from whom the faithful receive rest, peace, and refreshing against all the hot persecutions of the world, the fiery temptations of Satan, and the burning heat of guiltiness for sin. They are burnt by the heat of the sun and may find refreshment, sustenance, and comfort in him, by the shadow of a tree: *"Under his shadow had I delight, and sat down,"* (Song of Solomon 2:3).

In the Old Testament, there are many shadows, containing only dark resemblances and types of heavenly things. But David is looking to a place which, in its fulfillment, is found in Christ. Christ is the mercy seat; he is the bread, he is the Word, he is the resurrection and the life, he is the direction for sincere pilgrims in this world and a rod of correction for those sons that need chastising.

In the time of the Gospel, in which Christ and all spiritual blessings in him are clearly and plainly *manifested*, one finds that Christ the mercy seat is the go-between—the One between the glory of God above the mercy seat and the wings that outstretch it, where one would be safe in its shadow.

One cannot look at a shadow and find all the details of everything they would like. Shadows make things hidden.

Such details cannot be perceived in a shadow—the distinct parts of a body, the eyes, the face, hands, and such things. The shadow tells a person that there is a body, but a clear image has all the lines, proportions, and details, which shadows lack. In the Law, they had a sight of Christ, yet it was darkly in a shadow, and under such a shadow is found protection, as David sought. But it is set under the mercy seat—the Christ—where Christians have the very express form and image of Christ with all his benefits.

What is found under the mercy seat but a shadow, a refuge, where the mercy seat casts a shadow in relation to the glory of God hovering above it? There, in such a shadow—a shadow created by the mercy seat—is found the protection of Almighty God, under which his people (as it were) are hid and kept safe. As Naomi said to Ruth, *"Under whose wings thou art come to trust,"* (Ruth 2:12), metaphorically referring to the ark of the covenant.

Angels demonstrate their great readiness to perform the will of God with all speed and haste. *"Every one had six wings,"* (Isaiah 6:2). They speedily work for the glory of God and use their entire being for the declaration of his holiness. Christ rides on the wings of the cherubim, and under him is found refuge and safety.

The Lord Jesus furthers this idea of the wings under which one is covered and protected by speaking to the common people of his day in a similitude of protection. As when a chicken hides her young under her *wings* (Matthew 23:37), so by these pictures, the Lord hides his church under the wings of his protection and mercy, where they may hide safely until the danger is passed—also being a common reference, an agricultural one, for the mercy seat.

The problem, as it pertains to the idea here, is that protection from common things is not merely the issue; and being in the mere shadow of something would not be able to help a physical problem. It is true that David was looking for God to be helpful to him and keep him and bring him to a strong tower and high rock, a place of good offense against danger. But that quickly changes into finding that place where he does not need to repeatedly run to but rather simply reside under.

To be in the shadow of his wings, to be in the shadow of the mercy seat, to reside there, to stay there, to be safe there for all time—it is a spiritual place. *"I will reside in the shadow of thy wings forever."* It is because the eternal covenant of God—the sure mercies of David—are found in the shadow of the throne of Christ, the ark of God, where his glory dwells unhindered, and his people are safe in the shadow of his mercy; which then assumes the humble station of those lying at his feet in his shadow.

Where does the Christian go for protection, help, or aid? Hebrews directs that he goes to the throne of God, to the mercy seat, where the glory dwells, where Christ is found, where the blood of sprinkling is found. The place of refuge where Christians are urged and directed to go is the *"throne of grace."* Christ has a throne, and his ark is his throne, and the place of his residing in heaven is a throne, and he sits on the throne of his Father at the Father's right hand. It is the place of his holiness and majesty, by way of *metonymy*.

Why is the mercy seat now *not* just simply called a mercy seat but *a throne of grace*? It is described as such because God's grace in Christ there accompanies his glorious majesty and holiness in its fulness. Holiness, majesty, and mercy all intermingle there; it is called *atonement*. It is the place where the sinner can find God's favor. The psalmist was determined to reside at such a place forever. It is the place that men may come into the holiest of holy places and approach God, but God through the Mediator. God on the throne, his glory above the throne, the angels carrying him from place to place on such a glorious throne, and yet, whithersoever he goes, the saints follow in his shadow. Such a place of refuge and that strong tower, that place of comfort and protection from the wrath and glory of God, is to consider the mercy of Christ.

What shall they obtain in the shadow of his wings, in the place of his majesty and holiness? Christians are directed to go to this shadowy place, this hidden spot, right at the submissive feet of the One sitting on the throne, to find grace to help in time of need. And even with boldness they go—not merely with trepidation as the High Priest did in the Old Testament, wondering if he would escape that holy place alive. Because going to a place of protection, as the psalmist said, was a good place, a place of refuge, a place he wanted to be for all time. Having such access to Christ is advantageous.

Access to God is fellowship with God. Access is happiness. Happiness is found in his holiness. His holiness is found in his work, at his throne, in all he did in fulfilling all the types for his people—that they may come into the clear manifestation of his work and hide in the shadow of his wings under his sprinkled blood, in atonement.

What benefits, then, are found at such a place of hiding at the mercy seat? It is easy to consider this, as it has been in the last few parts of this study: to find mercy at the mercy seat and grace there to help in time of need. Mercy to pity undeserving sinners, and grace to help those who are unable to help themselves. Such a throne, by way of metonymy, is set down for all the advantages and benefits which are found in Jesus Christ and the blood of his sprinkling.

Why would the psalmist go anywhere else? Mercy looks at sinners as pitiable. Grace looks at them as undeserving. So in both, it shows forth the work of the Mediator that is housed in the love and compassion he has for those undeserving sinners whom he pities. Did David want mercy from God? Did David desire God's grace? So much so that it was under the shadow of his wings, in that place alone, in which he would find all respite—and that forever.

He did not need to go from place to place. He did not need to wander around to find something better and better. What does he look to but what God has prescribed, what God has set up, what God has done in salvation—forever. There is no need to go anywhere else and find anything else. David knew that such a place of mercy and grace, in the shadow of his wings, there in the most holy of all places, where the Redeemer sat on his throne, was a place he must consider in two parts.

The first part is that he needed mercy and grace and so considered himself a sinner in God's eye. Not that he could do anything, or bring anything. What would he bring into the shadow of the mercy seat? He could not bring gifts—what gift would he bring? He could not bring blood—that had already been sprinkled in sacrifice. He could not bring any kind of liveliness, for he knew that God was the one who held all life in his hands. He could not add to any of God's words, for God is the Word of life and in the ark of the testimony was his word already set down. He could not plead some measure of greatness in his kingship— God already had a crown on his ark, in which the golden emblems of holiness were found set in the glory of the cherubim.

Was David discouraged coming with nothing? Was David put off in coming without being able to add anything? Was David put off because he was a sinner? He set his eyes on his sin, and yet, at the very same time, he looked to the shadow—that cool place of refreshing where he could find mercy and grace from God. Interestingly, he knew that what he sought there would be there, and that forever. He wanted to be in the shadow of the mercy seat for all time. Does not this argue greatly for God's desire to bless his people? Does not this argue greatly for God's readiness in looking to bestow and cultivate and stir up and motion sinners to understand and see and experience the entirety of the

Chapter 8: The Wings

spiritual blessings they have in Christ? Do sinners need help? *Where does my help come from?*

David was persuaded, by the Spirit in him, that God is ready to forgive, to help, to comfort, to bless, to aid, to set one high upon a rock, to bring them into a strong tower, to set them in the shadow of the place they can find mercy and grace. William Gouge said, *"This also may be a motive to stir us up to cry and call to God in all our distresses. Children in their need will cry to their parents, yet it may be their parents hear them not; or if they hear them, are not able to help them; as Hagar could not help her child, Gen. 21:16. But God always hears, even our inward cries, Exod. 14:15."*[19] Christ is called the Sun of Righteousness. One might wonder how that applies to the mercy seat and the shadows. *"But unto you that fear my Name, shall the Sun of Righteousness arise with healing in his wings,"* (Malachi 4:2). This is spoken about Jesus Christ, which the prophet is explaining. Christ is the bright and shining sun of righteousness—why then does the prophet say something about wings? Why does a shining sun need wings?

Plainly, from the scope and context of the prophet, he is speaking about the Savior and his mercy, and that which will come in Gospel times. Christ is compared to the rising of the bright sun from a dark night. Certainly, the Gospel speaks to that—but what of these wings?

---

[19] William Gouge, *A Learned and Very Useful Commentary on the Whole Epistle to the Hebrews* (London: A.M., T.W. and S.G. for Joshua Kirton, 1655), 469.

When Christ fulfills all that he comes to fulfill, as the great brilliance of the Father, the great exegete of the Father to declare him to the world as he did, being the bright and morning star, there must be a refuge to run to, and it is the refuge where wings are found. If Christ comes to demonstrate the righteousness of God the Father as a Sun shining brilliantly all over the face of the whole earth, men will run and hide themselves from the holiness of God under fig leaves and mountains, and they run to the wrong place.
In the shadow of his wings there is found refuge. Not away from him, but up close and personal to him—in the shadow of his throne, in submission at his feet, in the shadow of the wings of the crown he bears and sits on at the ark. This is why Christ is the Mediator, the one who intervenes between sinners and his holiness. He must cast the shadow from his work over them, that they would be safe in the shadow of the ark. *"The LORD is thy keeper: the LORD is thy shade upon thy right hand,"* (Psalm 121:5).

God's love and protection in Christ to miserable sinners is found under the shadow of the mercy seat. Sin is of such a defiling nature that it is called *uncleanness,* and such is not hidden from the sight of God's holiness. Holiness cries out against the heinous nature of sin. And yet, one finds at the mercy seat—mercy, love, the exceeding greatness of God's love in Christ. There, of all places, at his throne, where the scepter of the love of Christ is held forth to miserable sinners. Because of that sprinkled blood, God's people may come to such a place—a throne—and never lack that which is needful for cleansing from sin and protection from his wrath. What, then, is the inexcusable nature of those who die in their sin and filthiness, after the Sun of Righteousness has come with healing in his wings, and yet they will not come to that throne, and they will not set themselves in submission to his will?

David knew the place of protection is the place of refuge, which is the mercy seat, the throne of Christ, where Christ's blood is sprinkled and forever will keep him safe. There are no other mercy seats. There is only one place where the love of the Father is found, and that is in Christ. There is no other blood of sprinkling, no other throne, no other golden scepter.

All soul-cleansing and soul-protecting is by Christ's blood. It is a throne to go boldly to. There Christ is willing for all who thirst, for all who come, for all who see need, to come and thirst and be filled. He will accept and embrace poor sinners. And it shows the very clear readiness of Christ for access to sinners, to find love and mercy.

Consider the multitude of sinners that have come to this throne and found mercy and love. Consider the multitude of sins in every one sinner that has been mercifully forgiven at this throne. Consider the happy state of all such as are made holy at this holy place—the most holy place of all places—where Christ sits and reigns.

Constant Persuasion to Go to the Right Place, with a Right Assurance

To know and believe that such a place exists is by divine intervention. The natural man does not come to Christ and has no need, he thinks, of the throne of mercy and grace. No need for a covering. No need to be hidden in his shadow. People often think that all they need to get to heaven is to be *dead*. They die, they go to heaven—most think. This is to undervalue the throne of grace by an infinite degree, and it is to slight the blood of sprinkling and the everlasting covenant.

The saved sinner, the converted sinner, has an infallible certainty by faith of their own salvation, and of the promise of grace, that such a place of mercy is very needful; and that such a place is only at Christ's throne, only at the Ark, only in the shadow of the mercy seat. It is a place you would dwell forever, as David would. *"Let us draw near with a true heart in full assurance of faith, having our hearts sprinkled from an evil conscience,"* (Heb. 10:22). You see the words continue in Hebrews, time and time again, to show forth the use of Old Testament types to New Testament thoughts. It is at that place that you find the mercy of Christ and the love of the Father. There is no other place for it to be found. Such an assurance of what Christ did is spiritual, which applies itself to your soul's safety; and later will transform your soul and body into a glorious soul and body to behold him as he is in heaven, in all his glory.

In the hope of Christ, and the truth of the Gospel of God, you have hope, faith, and delight in such spiritual things now; it is the place you desire to be forever. Many people desire heaven in a carnal and temporary way to be rid of the difficulties of life. Life is hard, so they want to go to heaven to escape that which is hard. The Christian considers heaven, in light of being fully satisfied in the work of Christ. It certainly has connotations of no pain, no more death, deliverance from sin, and such, but it is all about a spiritual persuasion of seeing Christ on his throne in the light of his glory forever and resting there in the place called *Ease* for all time.

You have a certain spiritual persuasion of such things as faith apprehends, to draw near and set yourself boldly at his throne, in the shadow of his wings, under the glory cloud of his work, under the blood of sprinkling now. Faith is that grace by which you approach God with a knowledge that you are accepted on account of the Son of Righteousness. Not that you accepted him, but that he accepts you.

You have a spiritual persuasion of your own salvation by Christ, *"Being fully persuaded that, what he had promised, he was able also to perform,"* (Rom. 4:21), being assured, *"That their hearts might be comforted, being knit together in love, and unto all riches of the full assurance of understanding,"* (Col. 2:2), that he has saved you, which you have a sound belief and experience of day to day.

May you who truly believe in the Lord Jesus, and love him in sincerity, and look for grace boldly at his covenant throne, and endeavor to walk in all good conscience before him, be assured of such mercies and love from the Father through the Son in the Spirit, even now. Of course, for you who are in a state of grace, being enabled by the Spirit to know the importance and truth of such things, knowing they are freely given to you of the Father, may be assured of your salvation in Christ. He has placed you under the shadow of his wings. *"And hereby we do know that we know him, if we keep his commandments,"* (1 John 2:3).

A change is made in you, and holiness is important to you. Yes, Christ has so changed you that you may know you have eternal life. And such an assurance is always experienced as one resides in the shadow of the Almighty. It derives from the benefits of Christ's blood sprinkled on the Ark, the testimony of the Holy Spirit, witnessing with our spirits, that we are the children of God, (Rom. 8:16).

And you know this because this assurance is set down on the promises of God, who cannot lie, (Isa. 54:10; John 3:36), further because you are sealed with the Holy Spirit of promise, which is the earnest of their inheritance.

You are then exhorted to love him who has loved you first and given you a resting place where you find refuge. You are thankful, to believe, to be humble, and to submit before him at his throne, for his glory. When you think of pity, and love, and compassion, you are reminded of the Ark of the covenant, Christ's mercy seat, his throne, from which he dispenses mercy and love, in the shadow of his wings. He gives you protection, and there you think of Christ whose glory you participate in by being shaded in his comfort.

There is a great consolation in this. This is why David had great peace to think that, at the place of shadows would be his consolation. There is a great comfort for you in this, a place that you could dwell forever in the shadow of his wings. Christ is more able to cleanse you by his blood than your sins could ever keep you off from receiving mercy. David would never be found to say that his sin could keep God from granting him comfort and mercy; he would not look for mercy and love in any other place. That his sin was greater than God was a Savior is unthinkable, which is why he wanted to reside in the shadow of the throne of God forever.

There is a great caution in this as well because you must take heed not to undervalue or slight what can be found at the mercy seat. You cannot undervalue what can be found in the shadow of his wings or think that it is such an open throne that it does not matter how you come or what you say, that God is some kind of cosmic bellhop to cater to your whims. Many people will try and rely on the benefits without ever considering what it took to get such benefits. They will rely on their hope of the mercy of Christ without having an eye and respect to Christ's blood or really having an eye on his throne; they hope in hope.

When all kinds of difficulties came upon the church, Phinehas' wife in 1 Samuel 4:19-22 saw the glory of God, the place of assurance, gone when the ark was taken. *"And she named the child Ichabod, saying, The glory is departed from Israel (because the ark of God was taken, and because of her father-in-law, and her husband.),"* (1 Sam. 4:21). The glorious type and assurance of God's presence, the Ark, which is often called God's glory, (Psalm 26:8, 78:61; Isa. 64:11), which was the ornament of mercy and the great protection of the church because it was the place where God dwelt above the cherubim, which they could glory in above all other nations—when it was no longer there, the glory of God was departed, and it seemed then, there was no place to find mercy and love.

What power could come against and destroy the souls who are sheltered in the ark of our salvation? Paul asks, *"Who can lay anything to the charge of God's elect?"* Christ has a mercy seat for them, he has died for them, and the Father has justified them.

What a happy assurance this is, where the ark perpetually sits at the right hand of the Father in heaven; where Christ is seated forever on such a throne, and Christians desire to dwell in its safety. What a grand picture of salvation to have Christ set his people in the ark, and make them safe under the shadow of his wings because of his blood, where he sits and reigns, and there, daily, they may go boldly to find grace, mercy, and love from the Father. You as Christians are all safe, so surely as you are in the Ark of the covenant, the ark of his love, covered in the blood of mercy, and the mercy seat itself. Under the mercy seat, there, safe under the shadow of those wings of cherubim. It is because God's love and protection in Christ to miserable sinners is found under the mercy seat.

God's Love and Protection in Christ is Found Under the Mercy Seat

The mercy *seat* (*i.e.* throne) was set on top of the ark of the covenant, which presses you to consider that mercy looks down from above, and it protects the law, though it applies the blood. Such mercy must be in Christ, even though the law stands to condemn, yet Christ has fulfilled it for sincere believers, that they may be justified in him and sanctified by his word.

Outside of Christ, the Ark and its contents are terrible things. The law is condemning because sinful men cannot uphold it. But at the throne of grace, at the Ark, Christ answers all the law for them, and for all their sins, so that they can come to God for mercy by him—splashed with blood. *"For Christ is the end of the law for righteousness to every one that believeth,"* (Rom. 10:4). And since you know that to be true, you do not come to the law without the mercy seat.

You come by the Ark, yet under the shadow of his wings. You come for grace, you come for love and mercy, you come to the Father for mercy by the Ark, by Christ, under the shadow of his wings. Grace originates and is poured down from the mercy seat to us, from above the mercy seat where the glory dwells, so that the mercy seat rests on the Ark in which you are safe.

So, sinners who see their need come to the Ark of Christ, his throne of grace, for mercy. And if you come to the Ark and are resting within it, under the mercy seat, and see the law, it does you no harm because Christ has covered you. Shadows are a sure sign of his glory there. Now it will only do you good, to direct you as to what will be sanctifying to you as you walk step by step before him.

This is why Hebrews will encourage you to have assurance, but to boldly come to such a throne, this mercy seat, to *"obtain mercy, and find grace to help in time of need,"* (Heb. 4:16). It is only here that you can see how the Father can accept you, and bestow blessings on you, to give you life, sustenance, direction, mercy, and love. The Ark shows you the reason for such things in Christ. It is there that you see how a just God can be merciful to you, and forgive you, and cleanse you, and make you happy, and that in a way of mercy, with one that has sinned against him. It is because all that the Father required of you, Christ has kept for you. The mercy seat sits on the Ark of the covenant, and so the Father acts in that perfect way of love and mercy, the way of grace toward you. This is because God's love and protection in Christ to miserable sinners is found under the mercy seat. And what is found there? Holiness. *Holiness* is found there, given for the whole of Christ's work—*holiness under the mercy seat*—which we will consider in our last chapter.

Chapter 9: The Holy Way

Hebrews 9:14, "How much more shall the blood of Christ, who through the eternal Spirit offered himself without spot to God, purge your conscience from dead works to serve the living God?"

The Priesthood of Christ, according to Hebrews, is central to the grand scheme of God's *covenant*, as the word of the *new* Testator who has come to finalize the *testament*. In the older administration of the covenant, Moses was the intermediary—a messenger, a prophet, informing the church of God's dealings with them and, the manner in which he would speak to them. But Moses knew that another would come in whom the people of God would listen (Deut. 18:15).

In this old covenant, there were holy ordinances and signifiers that pointed forward to this coming Mediator. The most important of these types was the Holy of Holies, where the ark of the covenant was set, containing the manna, the rod, and the covenant tablets. Over this ark was set the mercy seat, the visible token of God's mercy to sinners. Above the mercy seat dwelt the presence of God in the glory cloud. This was the most holy place—an enclosed, sacred chamber, without windows to gaze outward, no distractions, only the throne and the glory of God. There, once a year, the high priest would enter and sprinkle the blood of the sacrifice upon the mercy seat, for, *"without shedding of blood is no remission,"* (Heb. 9:22).

The writer of Hebrews highlights how these types are divided into two great works: atonement and intercession.

Christ as the Final Mediator: The Fulfillment of Atonement and Intercession

Jesus Christ, the final and true Mediator of the New Covenant, made atonement to satisfy divine justice (1 John 2:2) and now continues his intercession in heaven (Heb. 9:14). He has secured his rightful place of power at the right hand of the Father, having made atonement to purge the conscience of his people from dead works, that they may serve the living God. His work of intercession is done in the *most* holy place—not an earthly sanctuary, but the very throne room of heaven. The types of the old covenant were mere *pictures* of what was to come. The ark, the tabernacle, the mercy seat, and the cherubim all pointed to the heavenly reality, but they were mere sketches compared to the glorious truth.

To use an illustration: imagine a beautifully painted landscape of a mountain. It may capture its beauty to some extent, but it cannot compare to standing, in the midst of that mountain range, breathing its air, feeling its height, and experiencing its grandeur firsthand. Such is the difference between the Old Testament types and the fulfillment of those types in Christ.

The Superiority of Christ over the Types is evident. The ark in the temple must be seen in lieu of the Christ in Heaven. The earthly ark was overlaid with gold; the heavenly throne is filled with the dazzling glory of the King of Kings. The ark had golden cherubim overshadowing it; in heaven, Christ is attended by angels worshiping in his presence. The ark was crowned with gold; Christ wears the crown of righteousness and dominion. The ark held tokens of God's provision—the manna, the rod, and the covenant tablets; Christ is the true Bread of Life, the resurrection and the life, and the living Word.

The mercy seat is the Throne of Christ. The mercy seat was the place where blood was sprinkled; Christ himself is the sacrifice, seated on the throne, as the Lamb slain from the foundation of the world. The mercy seat was a token of God's mercy; Christ is the fulfillment of that mercy.

The Day of Atonement must be considered in light of Christ's finished work. The priest entered once a year to offer sacrifices repeatedly; Christ, by his one sacrifice, *"hath perfected forever them that are sanctified,"* (Heb. 10:14). The priest could only enter with fear and trembling; Christians now *boldly* approach the throne of grace (Heb. 4:16).

The effects of Christ's atonement prove its sufficiency: Reconciliation with God (Col. 1:20), the appeasing of divine wrath (2 Cor. 5:21), the full expiation and pardon of sin (1 John 1:7), the eternal redemption of God's elect (Rom. 3:24, 5:10; Heb. 1:3, 9:14, 10:14). If the atonement of Christ were not *complete*, none of these blessings could be obtained. If he were not fit for the task, he could not *accomplish* them. But being the eternal Mediator, he has done this work to the uttermost, securing salvation for all who come to God by him (Heb. 7:25).

The Purging of the Conscience: From Dead Works to Living Worship

Hebrews 9:14 teaches that through Christ's atonement, the conscience is *purged* from dead works. A defiled conscience is a burden, for a man under guilt is always a man under judgment. He feels the weight of his sins, unable to cleanse himself, and is condemned before God's holy law. But Christ, by his atoning blood, purges the conscience from dead works so that the believer might serve the living God. What are dead works? These are not merely sinful acts but also vain religious efforts done apart from Christ. The old sacrifices were dead works—repeated, yet never able to take away sins (Heb. 10:1-4). Human righteousness is a dead work—*"all our righteousnesses are as filthy rags,"* (Isa. 64:6). Any effort to justify oneself before God outside of Christ is a dead work—*"For by the works of the law shall no flesh be justified,"* (Gal. 2:16). The atonement of Christ not only removes guilt but transforms the sinner. Where once he sought refuge in dead works, now he serves the living God with a new and living faith. As William Perkins writes: *"Christian liberty and certainty of salvation are the properties of a purged conscience. The conscience is only truly freed when it finds its rest in the blood of Christ."*[20]

Hebrews 9:14 connects God's attributes with *service in worship. He is the living God; therefore, we must render to him a living service.* He is the living God—our worship must be lively. The service of believers is not a cold, lifeless ritual, but an active, spiritual worship. Just as Christ was raised from the dead, so are his people raised to newness of life. Service to God is not burdensome but joyous—*"Serve the Lord with gladness,"* (Psa. 100:2).

He sits on his throne, attended by cherubim. His throne is mobile, carried by the wings of angels (Ezek. 1:10-28). His saints *follow* him wherever he goes (Rev. 14:4). They serve in submission under his mercy, covered in the blood of sprinkling.

This service is through the triune God. The Father planned redemption. The Son accomplished redemption. The Spirit applies redemption. The believer, therefore, serves God in the power of the Spirit, through the Son, to the glory of the Father.

The Greatness of Christ's Atonement

The atonement of Christ is more than a mere theological concept—it is the foundation of all true worship

---

[20] William Perkins, *The Works of William Perkins*, ed. J. Stephen Yuille, Joel R. Beeke, and Derek W. H. Thomas, vol. 8 (Grand Rapids, MI: Reformation Heritage Books, 2019), 56–57.

and service to God. It cleanses the conscience, removes dead works, and brings believers into living *communion* with the living God. Why would anyone look anywhere else? The lesser has given way to the greater. The shadow has given way to the reality. The blood of bulls and goats has given way to the blood of the Lamb.

Christ reigns at the right hand of the Father—his work is finished, and his throne is a throne of mercy. *"How much more shall the blood of Christ... purge your conscience from dead works to serve the living God?"* Let every redeemed sinner come boldly to his mercy seat and serve him in holiness and joy, from this time forth and even forevermore.

Doctrine: God's gracious bestowal of mercy in Christ tends to *holy practice*.

The power of the truth is bound up in the Word of God itself, and it would be no true doctrine without it. Scripture is the foundation of every line, every argument, every truth put forward here. The error of many is to lean on their own reasoning, thinking they might build a house of faith without the stones of God's own Word. But such a house will fall, for it lacks a sure foundation. So, let us bring back the Scripture in its rightful place that the doctrine may stand firm and unmoved.

God's gracious bestowal of mercy in Christ is no *idle* thing. It does not merely rescue a man from the fire—it sets his feet on solid ground and bids him walk uprightly. True faith, an earnest faith, leads to godly living. It cannot do otherwise. It is "faith which worketh by love," (Gal. 5:6).

Chapter 9: The Holy Way

The 1647 Westminster Confession declares that the perseverance of the saints is "upon the efficacy of the merit and intercession of Jesus Christ."[21] His intercession is not a passive thing, not a mere formality. It is the active and living plea of the great High Priest, who ever lives to make intercession for his people, (Heb. 7:25). And as the Larger Catechism wisely states, the Mediator had to be God so that he might "give worth and efficacy to his sufferings, obedience, and intercession ... and bring them to everlasting salvation."

If a man has truly laid hold of Christ, if he has been brought to kneel beneath the mercy seat, washed in the blood of the covenant, then he is *changed*. His heart is new, his conscience is clean, and he is no longer what he was. The Gospel does not merely offer an escape—it offers Christ. It offers a Redeemer who fulfills every type, every shadow, every ordinance that once pointed toward him. It is not that these old things were done away with in the sense of being discarded; rather, they are fulfilled so completely in Christ that nothing else remains but to look to him alone. And so, with a conscience purged from dead works, the believer is made fit to serve the living God, (Heb. 9:14).

A good conscience walks in step with the Spirit, "the spirit of wisdom and understanding, the spirit of counsel and might, the spirit of knowledge and of the fear of the LORD," (Isa. 11:2). It is no longer accused, no longer trembling under the weight of past sins, for Christ has taken

---

[21] *1647 Westminster Confession of Faith* 17:2.

them away, (1 John 1:7). An evil conscience, however, remains restless, tormented by sin, still carrying the guilt it was never meant to bear, for "there is no peace, saith my God, to the wicked," (Isa. 57:21). But Christ has purified the conscience of his people, "for if our heart condemn us, God is greater than our heart, and knoweth all things," (1 John 3:20).

Christ is not merely a Savior in name—he is the Messiah, the fulfillment of every prophecy, the promised seed who would crush the serpent's head, (Gen. 3:15). He is the Lamb slain from the foundation of the world, (Rev. 13:8), the suffering servant who bore the iniquities of many, (Isa. 53:11). There is no other name under heaven given among men whereby we must be saved, (Acts 4:12). And what kind of salvation does he bring? A partial one? A weak one? No, it is a complete salvation, for "he is able also to save them to the uttermost that come unto God by him," (Heb. 7:25). His obedience is both active and passive. By his active obedience, he fulfilled the Law completely, "when the fulness of the time was come, God sent forth his Son, made of a woman, made under the law," (Gal. 4:4). By his passive obedience, he bore the punishment of the Law for those who could not, satisfying the justice of God, (Rom. 5:19).

And what does this salvation lead to? A life of ease, free from all duty? No, it leads to a life of service. Christ himself declared, "If any man will come after me, let him deny himself, and take up his cross daily, and follow me," (Luke 9:23). To be saved by Christ is to be called into his service, to serve the living God. What does that mean? It means holiness.

Holiness is not a mere moral striving; it is the reflection of God's own character. "Be ye holy; for I am holy," (1 Pet. 1:16). It is the disposition of the heart that loves what God loves and hates what God hates. "I have sworn once by my holiness," says the Lord, "that I will not lie unto David," (Psa. 89:35). His holiness is his very being, and those whom he saves are called into that holiness.

Yet holiness is not a thing that men achieve by effort—it is wrought in them by the Spirit. The Holy Spirit makes the people of God holy by applying to them the benefits of Christ's work. And where do they find this holiness? At the mercy seat. The writer of Hebrews bids them to come boldly to the throne of grace, that they may obtain mercy and find grace to help in time of need, (Heb. 4:16). And when is their time of need? Is it not always? Every day, every hour, they are in need, and so they must go continually to that throne, to the shadow of the Almighty, (Psa. 91:1).

This is the place where holiness is found, where the believer's heart is shaped into the likeness of his Savior. Holiness is no mere external thing—it is the inward purity that makes a man truly righteous. "And that ye put on the new man, which after God is created in righteousness and true holiness," (Eph. 4:24). It is the mark of those who are truly his, for "without holiness no man shall see the Lord," (Heb. 12:14). It is not optional. It is not an extra blessing for a few. It is the *necessary fruit* of salvation.

And so the believer, having been made clean by the blood of Christ, does not shrink back. He comes to the mercy seat, reminded of what lies beneath it—the tablets of the Law, the manna, the rod that budded—and he sees their fulfillment in Christ. He sees the Law kept in perfection, the Bread of Life given for his sustenance, the rod of resurrection declaring victory over death. And he serves. He serves the living God, not out of fear, not as a slave, but as a son.

Holiness is the *heart* of worship. It is what God requires in all who come near him. "I will be sanctified in them that come nigh me, and before all the people I will be glorified," (Lev. 10:3). True worship is not a mere outward form—it is a life set apart for God. "But now being made free from sin, and become servants to God, ye have your fruit unto holiness, and the end everlasting life," (Rom. 6:22). Holiness is not only the way to God—it is the evidence that one has been brought to him.

So then, let no man think he can claim Christ and yet live unchanged. Holiness is the necessary fruit of mercy. It is not the price of salvation, but it is the proof of it. And those who have been made clean by the blood of Christ, will long to serve him, not out of compulsion, but out of love. For they know what has been done for them, and they know that they have been set free—set free to be holy, set free to be his. And so they come, boldly, continually, not with fear, but with joy, for they know that the throne of grace is their home, the mercy seat their refuge, and Christ himself their all in all.

Chapter 9: The Holy Way

To come before God in worship is no light thing. It is not a casual matter, as if a man might saunter into the courts of heaven with dust on his boots and sin on his breath, expecting to be received as an honored guest. No, if there is one thing made plain from the first pages of Genesis to the last echoes of Revelation, it is that God is holy, and those who come near to Him must be holy too. "Holiness becometh thy house, O Lord, forever," (Psa. 93:5).

Where then should a man go, and how should he come? He must come under the mercy seat, under the shadow of the Almighty, with a conscience purified, washed in the blood of Christ, so that his worship might be acceptable. For without such a purification, his worship is defiled, his prayers are polluted, and his very presence is an offense. "*To the pure all things are pure, but unto them that are defiled and unbelieving is nothing pure,*" (Titus 1:15). It is a wonder that many do not consider this. They come before God without thought, without care, without preparation, as though He were some common acquaintance. They are not careful to bring a sanctified heart before Him in worship, nor do they tremble at His word.

This is a grave mistake, for to neglect God's prescribed worship is *to depart from Him entirely*. False worship is not just an error—it is the great sin of all mankind, the root from which idolatry, superstition, and apostasy all spring. "*Thou shalt worship the Lord thy God, and him only shalt thou serve,*" (Matt. 4:10). This is no mere outward form, no lifeless ceremony. It must be true worship, the honor of a renewed heart, loving, fearing, and trusting in

God because of His infinite knowledge, mercy, and power. *"They that worship him must worship him in spirit and in truth,"* (John 4:24).

A man cannot bring *unclean* worship to a holy God. What folly is it to suppose that the Lord who demanded the spotless lamb under the Law will now receive polluted sacrifices in the Gospel? Under the old covenant, if a man came to offer a sacrifice while in his uncleanness, he was to be cut off. Yet many today seem to believe that God has grown lenient, that He will wink at their sins, that He will take whatever worship they offer, no matter how defiled it may be. It is not so. They flatter themselves. They forget that God is "of purer eyes than to behold evil," (Hab. 1:13).

No one should dare to offer unclean worship. There is no coming to God without washing, without being made clean, for "Holiness becometh thy house, O Lord, forever," (Psa. 93:5). And how is this cleansing accomplished? By purging. "And purge us to be a peculiar people," (Titus 2:14). To be purged is to be made clean, to have guilt removed through the forgiveness of sins, through the blood of Christ. It is to have the heart washed from the corruption of sin so that it does not reign, that it does not have dominion over the soul. "Purge your heart, you sinners," (James 4:8). This is no passive work, no idle wish—it is an earnest endeavor, a casting out of filth, a striving for holiness so that God might be served rightly.

Dead works (*i.e.* things not prescribed by God) will never be accepted as worship. God is the living God, and He must be worshiped with living hearts, with living faith, with living sacrifice accordingly. *"Present your bodies a living sacrifice, holy, acceptable unto God, which is your reasonable service,"* (Rom. 12:1). There is no room for dead worship, no room for vain words and empty rituals. Sanctification consists in both the killing of sin and the new life that flows from beneath the mercy seat. In the Old Testament, every sacrifice was to be seasoned with salt, to show that sin must be put to death when one comes to worship the living God. So too, when the Christian comes to offer himself to God, the grace of Christ must season him, the grace of God must mortify his lusts.

The conscience must be clean. "How much more shall the blood of Christ… purge your conscience from dead works to serve the living God?" (Heb. 9:14). If a man's conscience is dirty, if his heart is defiled, he cannot serve God rightly. He cannot offer true worship. He cannot even lift his voice in praise without offense. And how is the conscience purged from dead works? By being set under the mercy seat, under the blood of sprinkling, where grace and mercy are poured out in abundance.

Let no man deceive himself. If he claims to be a Christian, if he claims to worship God, let him first examine his own heart. Has the Spirit of Christ applied the atonement to his soul? Has he been washed, sanctified, and made new? If not, then his worship is no better than the vain offerings of Cain, no better than the incense of Nadab and Abihu, no better than the prayers of the Pharisee who trusted in himself. He may call himself a Christian, but if he does not worship with a purged conscience, he shows himself never to have been set under the mercy seat. He is not fed by Christ's sustenance, not enlivened by His resurrection power, not directed by His laws. "He that is not with me is against me," (Matt. 12:30).

Dead works have no place in the service of Christ. They are deadly things, bringing death upon the sinner who clings to them. "The blood of Christ cleanseth," (1 John 1:7). Not only from the guilt of sin in justification, but also from the power of sin in sanctification. Christ's atonement frees the sinner so that he might serve the living God. The death of Christ, applied to the soul by faith, brings a sin-killing virtue, a virtue that makes the believer dead to sin and alive to God.

This is the order of grace. First, to find grace under the mercy seat, then to live under the mercy seat, then to serve under the mercy seat. The Christian is one who has received the gift of spiritual life, and he is obliged to exercise it. "Giving all diligence, add to your faith virtue, and to virtue knowledge," (2 Pet. 1:5). There is no coasting, no laziness in the Christian life. They live to God, they worship Him in truth, they obey His word. "Blessed is the man that feareth God, that delighteth greatly in his commandments," (Psa. 112:1).

Their lives *answer* Christ's atonement. Even in their humility, even in their sense of unworthiness, they show forth the effect of grace. They do not come before the throne of grace casually. They do not come as beggars hoping for scraps. They come boldly, as those who have been granted access by the blood of Christ, "that we may obtain mercy, and find grace to help in time of need," (Heb. 4:16). But they come with reverence, with submission, with a heart bent toward obedience.

Many think of these verses only in terms of personal benefit. They think of the throne of grace as a place to have their problems solved, their burdens lifted, their prayers answered. They do not think of it as a place of *service*, a place where they must bow low in humility. They forget that to come to the mercy seat is to submit, to forsake sin, to put it to death once and for all. "Grace to help in time of need"—what does this mean? Does it mean grace for an easier life? Grace for a promotion? Grace for a new house? No. It means grace to walk in *holiness*, grace to *mortify* sin, grace to live in the *shadow* of the Almighty. This is the road of holiness, the narrow way that leads to eternal life. "When we live from an everlasting principle to an everlasting end, then we live to God as Christ did," (Thomas Manton). There is an order in grace, and there is an order in worship. And those who have been washed, who have been sanctified, who have been made new, will live as those who are truly under the mercy seat, truly under the shadow of His wings, truly under the blood of Christ.

What, then, *distresses the Christian most?* Is it the weight of the world pressing down upon him? The common hardships of life? The trials that rise up like waves upon the sea? No, if he is a true Christian, it is not these things that cut him deepest—it is his own *lack of holiness*, the great chasm that ever seems to lie between what he is and what he longs to be in Christ. He desires to be holy, yet he sees his failings. He strains forward, yet stumbles. He yearns for godliness, yet finds himself still tied to the wretched weight of sin.

David Brainerd, a man deeply acquainted with his own soul's struggle, lamented, "I was distressed to think that I should offer such dead cold services to the living God! My soul seemed to breathe after holiness, a life of constant devotedness to God. But I am almost lost sometimes in the pursuit of this blessedness, and ready to sink, because I continually fall short and miss of my desire. Oh, that the Lord would help me to hold out, yet a little while, till the happy hour of deliverance comes."[22] This was the cry of a man who understood the holiness of God and trembled at the thought of offering up cold worship. But is it the cry of Christians today? Is it your cry? Do you groan for holiness? Does your heart burn with the desire to be made pure? Or have modern Christians so dulled their consciences that such thoughts never trouble them?

There is no lack of *means* for holiness. The Christian lacks nothing that God has not already provided. The mercy seat has been opened, the throne of grace has been set before him, and all who thirst are bid to come and drink freely. Yet how few come earnestly! How many linger in their own strength, attempting to manufacture holiness as if it were a thing to be produced by human effort! It is Christ who is the fountain of all righteousness, and He pours out His grace as it pleases Him. What He wills to be done shall be done, yet

---

[22] Jonathan Edwards, *The Life of David Brainerd*, ed. Norman Pettit and John E. Smith, Corrected Edition, vol. 7, *The Works of Jonathan Edwards* (New Haven; London: Yale University Press, 2002), 171.

He has given you a throne to come to, a mercy seat beneath which you may set yourself and be safe.

Knowing this, Christians ought to carefully observe the means God has provided for living to Him. He has not left us to stumble blindly. He has given His Word to be read, His Gospel to be preached, His sacraments to be received, and prayer to be the ever-flowing conversation between the soul and its Maker. He has given catechesis, fasting, thanksgiving, and worship as a regular part of Christian life. And yet, many approach these things as if they were trivial—as if God's holiness were a light thing. They do not see that all of life is worship. They do not understand that every thought, every action, every moment is lived before the face of God.

Theology itself is nothing less than the doctrine of living to God. William Ames rightly defined it as "the doctrine of living to God."[23] It is not merely the study of doctrine for doctrine's sake, nor an intellectual exercise to satisfy curiosity. It is the knowledge of God that leads to the worship of God. If your theology does not press you to greater holiness, if it does not drive you to love Christ more and hate sin more, then it is not true theology.

But there are many who are *religious* without being regenerate. There are many who are awakened in part, but never fully. They hear of Christ, but they do not know Him.

---

[23] William Ames quoted in Richard A. Muller, *Post-Reformation Reformed Dogmatics: The Rise and Development of Reformed Orthodoxy; Volume 1: Prolegomena to Theology*, 2nd ed. (Grand Rapids, MI: Baker Academic, 2003), 155.

They read of holiness, but they have never tasted it. They are like men who have read about the sweetness of honey but have never let it touch their tongues. Modern churches are *built* with such people. They will offer sacrifices, as Israel did—thousands of rams, rivers of oil, even the fruit of their bodies for the sin of their souls (Micah 6:6-7). They will do everything except what *God actually commands*. They think that *more* is better. They think that their own efforts can compensate for their sin. They are not familiar with the true cry of the soul: *"Turn us, O Lord God of hosts, cause thy face to shine; and we shall be saved,"* (Psalm 80:19).

The true Christian is not like this. He does not offer dead works. He does not bring his own righteousness before God, but instead, he theologically places himself under the mercy seat, under the blood of Christ. He has been given an interest in Christ, and because of this, he has been *made new*. His conscience, once darkened, is now purged. He serves the living God with the confidence that he is accepted in the Beloved. *"He hath translated us into the kingdom of his dear Son,"* (Colossians 1:13). This is the foundation upon which the Church is built (Matthew 16:16-18). The man who has been renewed by Christ cannot remain as he was. Holiness follows. It must follow.

God's gracious bestowal of mercy in Christ bends the will to holy practice. It presses the soul toward godliness. As William Ames put it, "Divinity is the doctrine of living to God. John 6:68, the words of eternal life. Acts 5:20, the words of this life. Rom. 6:11, Reckon yourselves to be alive to God."[24] To be alive to God is not merely a theological concept—it is a reality. It is the very essence of Christianity. A man who is truly alive to God cannot help but walk in holiness. He cannot help but long for righteousness.

Wilhelmus à Brakel gives the heart of the matter: "Since the Lord Jesus as my Surety has removed all my sin by His death, and as evidence of this has arisen from the dead, should I then yet live in sin? Should not I then arise with Him from the death of sin and live with Him in all holiness?"[25] Here is the Christian's great question: Shall I live in sin when Christ has died to free me from it? Shall I offer cold and dead worship when Christ has made me alive? Shall I drag myself through life as if grace were a burden, rather than a fountain of living water?

If you have been supernaturally born again, if you have been made alive in Christ, then your deepest desire must be to serve God in *righteousness* (Romans 6:3–11). You will not be content to live in mediocrity: *mediocre* church, *mediocre* devotions, *mediocre* morality. You will not be satisfied with *half-hearted* devotion. Your life will be marked by the *pursuit of holiness*. You will long to dwell in the holiest place of all places. You will seek to live under the shadow of the Almighty. You will press forward, even as you groan under the weight of your own imperfections. And as you do, you will rest in the knowledge that you are protected by

---

[24] William Ames, *The Marrow of Theology*, eBook, 1:1.
[25] Wilhelmus à Brakel, *The Christian's Reasonable Service*, vol. 1 (Morgan, PA: Soli Deo Gloria Publications, 1993), 634.

Christ, sanctified by His Spirit, and held fast by the mercy of God.

This is what it means to live under the mercy seat. It is to walk with God, as Adam once did in the cool of the day. It is to be hidden in the Rock, as Moses was. It is to dwell in the presence of the Most High, knowing that in Him alone is life, holiness, and joy everlasting.

God is a most gracious and bountiful Lord. He is not like the kings of the earth, who hoard their riches and dispense them only in measured portions, or like the men of commerce, who require an exchange before they will give. No, He fills all things with goodness and asks for no return but praise and thanksgiving. That is the whole of it. He pours out mercies upon mercies, and all He asks in response is that you acknowledge them, that you do not pass through life as an ungrateful beggar, consuming daily gifts and never lifting your eyes in thanks.

Do not defraud God of this *easy service*. Having been made a new creature in Him, should not your heart be ever filled with a sense of His kindness, and your mouth with the acknowledgment of His mercies? It is no burden to thank Him. It is no toil to praise Him. It is the very height of joy, the most pleasant and satisfying thing a soul can do. And yet, how often do men take His gifts with mute ingratitude, as if they owed Him nothing? How many live as if His kindness were merely their due, rather than an overwhelming act of grace?

Let it not be so with you. Every time you hear of His throne, think of the ark. Every time you hear of His protection, think of the shadow of His wings. Let your mind be drawn ever to the mercy seat, and let your heart be filled with affectionate devotion to the God who has set you beneath it. But do not be content with words alone. Offer up your thanks not only with your lips, but with your life. Show forth His praise by consecrating yourself to His service, by walking in holiness and righteousness before Him all your days, through Jesus Christ our Lord.

It is no small thing to walk in holiness. It is a great and glorious work, and one that cannot be done in human strength alone. But you are not left to yourself. Christ stands ever at the throne of grace, overshadowing you, protecting you, helping you to walk. You may boldly come for grace. You may stretch out your hands in need, and He will not turn you away. This is the mercy of God—to take sinful, broken men and lead them into holiness. He is not content merely to save them; He will sanctify them. He will cleanse them. He will lead them, step by step, until they reach His presence in glory.

And what is the aim of all this? That you may fear and reverence Him. That you may *serve* Him in worship. That you may renounce all ungodliness and worldly lusts, and walk in holiness of life, setting your hope upon the kingdom of heaven, where one day you will stand before the throne, not in shadow, but in sight. Christ did not die that you might wallow in sin. He did not shed His blood that you might live as you please. No, He came to destroy the kingdom of the devil, to break the chains of sin, and to make you holy. He came not only to obtain pardon for your sins, but to sanctify you, to dedicate you to the service of God. John Calvin put it well: "*Here we cannot be Christians without being new creatures (Eph. 2:2), formed unto good works, which God has prepared, in order that we should walk in them, seeing that of ourselves we would not be so disposed. But the will and execution are given us by God, and all our sufficiency is of Him (Phil. 2:13); and for this purpose our Lord Jesus Christ has received all fullness of grace, that we may draw from Him (2 Cor. 3:5).*"[26]

This is the Christian life: to be made a partaker of His blessings by faith, and to live in holiness as the fruit of that faith. But you know your own weakness. You know that, though redeemed to serve God in holiness and righteousness, you are pressed on all sides by temptations, by the weight of this fallen world, and by the weakness of your own flesh. You know how tainted your affections are, how blemished your thoughts, how even your best works are stained with impurity. You are constantly aware of how you fail Him. And yet, at the same time, you are safe in the ark. At the same time, you know that Christ has satisfied all things for you, so that you may grow in holiness and walk before God without fear.

Do not make excuses. There are no excuses for the Christian. There is no justification for half-hearted service. You have been given everything you need. You are safe in the ark, guided by His Word, nourished by His sustenance, led by His Spirit. If you fail, He will pick you up. If you stumble,

---

[26] John Calvin and Henry Beveridge, *Tracts Relating to the Reformation*, vol. 2 (Edinburgh: Calvin Translation Society, 1849), 144.

He will set you back on the way. He will keep you under the shadow of His wings. He will not cast you out.

Yet let there be a final warning. Do not be deceived. To *neglect* holiness as God prescribes is to *prove* that you are not in the ark at all. The man who takes no care for his soul, who does not strive to serve God in sincerity according to Christ's prescriptions, who does not pursue holiness—such a man shows himself to be a beast, dead to the things of God, neither feeling his need nor perceiving his danger. He walks carelessly into hell, as if in a dream, and there will be no waking from it.

Be earnest, then. Be sincere. Come before the throne of grace not merely in word, but in truth. Cry out that He would seal His free election in your heart by the Holy Spirit. Plead that He would shelter you under the shadow of His wings. Seek that Christ would keep you beneath the protection of His mercy seat, that you may be subject to His will and maintained by His power. The world, the flesh, and the devil will strive to shake you. They will try to pull you away. But rest in the shadow of His work. For *"The Lord knoweth them that are His,"* (2 Timothy 2:19).

And in this, you demonstrate whose you are. In this, you prove yourself a child of God. In this, you make it clear that you belong to Him. Do *not* depart from holiness. Do not drift from the mercy seat. Stand steadfast. Cling to Christ. Live in the shadow of His wings, and grow in grace, until that day when God takes you to His eternal kingdom, where at last, you will see the mercy seat with your own eyes, and dwell in His presence forever.

Other Works by Dr. McMahon at Puritan Publications

5 Marks of a Biblical Church

5 Marks of a Biblical Disciple

5 Marks of Biblical Commitment to the Visible Body of Christ

5 Marks of Biblical Reformation

5 Marks of Christian Resolve

5 Marks of Devotion to God

A Heart for Reformation

A Practical Guide to Primeval History

A Simple Overview of Covenant Theology

A Watchman Over Christ's Church

Augustine's Calvinism: The Doctrines of Grace in Augustine's Writings

Bah Humbug: How Christians Should Think About the Christmas Holiday

Being with Jesus

Christ Commanding His Coronavirus to Covenant Breakers

Chapter 9: The Holy Way

Christ the Apple Tree and the Joy of True Religion

Covenant Theology Made Easy

Eternity Weighed in the Balance

Following Christ Whithersoever He Goes

Gradual Reformation Intolerable

Historical Theology Made Easy

How Faith Works: Rescuing the Gospel from Contemporary Evangelicalism

How to Live Every Day in the End Times

I Am for You: God's Power in Supporting His People

John 3:16

John Calvin's View of God's Love and the Doctrine of Reprobation

Joseph's Resolve and the Unreasonableness of Sinning Against God

Overcoming Lust In a Sex-crazed World

Practical Observations on the Book of Ruth

Practical Observations on the Lord's Supper

Psalm 96: A Theology of Praise 2nd Edition

Reformation of the Heart, Soul and Mind

Save Me: A Study of Psalm 119:89-96

Seeing Christ Clearly

Sophia and the Umbrella – A Children's Book on Justification

Sparks of Divine Glory: A Practical Study of the Attributes of God

Systematic Theology Made Easy

The Cage: A Young Children's Guide to the Biblical Teaching on Hell

The Five Principles of the Gospel

The Kingdom of Heaven is Upon You

The Lord's Voice Cries to the City: A Biblical Guide for Hearing the Word of God Preached

The Reformation Made Easy

The Reformed Apprentice: A Workbook on Reformed Theology (Volumes 1-4)

The Ten Commandments in the Life of the Christian

The Two Wills of God Made Easy

The Two Wills of God: Does God Really Have Two Wills?

Chapter 9: The Holy Way

The Wickedness, Humiliation, Restoration and Reformation of Manasseh

Umiko and the Mask – Children's Book on Election

Underneath the Blood

Unmasking Self-Flattery in the Church

Walking Victoriously in the Power of the Spirit

www.ingramcontent.com/pod-product-compliance
Lightning Source LLC
Chambersburg PA
CBHW030855170426
43193CB00009BA/613